How to Open & Operate a Financially Successful Interior Design Business:

With Companion CD-ROM

By Diane Leone

D0109304

How to Open & Operate a Financially Successful Interior
Design Business: With Companion CD-ROM

Copyright © 2010 Atlantic Publishing Group, Inc.
1405 SW 6th Avenue • Ocala, Florida 34471 • Phone 800-814-1132 • Fax 352-622-1875
Web site: www.atlantic-pub.com • E-mail: sales@atlantic-pub.com
SAN Number: 268-1250

Library of Congress Cataloging-in-Publication Data

Leone, Diane., 1954-
  How to open & operate a financially successful interior design business : with companion
CD-ROM / by Diane Leone .
      p. cm.
  Includes bibliographical references and index.
  ISBN-13: 978-1-60138-262-7 (alk. paper)
  ISBN-10: 1-60138-262-6 (alk. paper)
  1. Interior decoration firms--Management. 2. Interior decoration--Practice. I. Title. II. Title:
How to open and operate a financially successful interior design business.
  NK2116.2.R87 2009
  747.068--dc22
                                        2008035792

Printed in the United States

PROJECT MANAGER: Melissa Peterson • mpeterson@atlantic-pub.com
ASSISTANT EDITOR: Angela Pham • apham@atlantic-pub.com
INTERIOR DESIGN: James Ryan Hamilton • www.jamesryanhamilton.com
COVER DESIGN: Meg Buchner • megadesn@mchsi.com
JACKET DESIGN: Jackie Miller • sullmill@charter.net

Printed on Recycled Paper

We recently lost our beloved pet "Bear," who was not only our best and dearest friend but also the "Vice President of Sunshine" here at Atlantic Publishing. He did not receive a salary but worked tirelessly 24 hours a day to please his parents. Bear was a rescue dog that turned around and showered myself, my wife, Sherri, his grandparents Jean, Bob, and Nancy, and every person and animal he met (maybe not rabbits) with friendship and love. He made a lot of people smile every day.

We wanted you to know that a portion of the profits of this book will be donated to The Humane Society of the United States. *–Douglas & Sherri Brown*

The human-animal bond is as old as human history. We cherish our animal companions for their unconditional affection and acceptance. We feel a thrill when we glimpse wild creatures in their natural habitat or in our own backyard.

Unfortunately, the human-animal bond has at times been weakened. Humans have exploited some animal species to the point of extinction.

The Humane Society of the United States makes a difference in the lives of animals here at home and worldwide. The HSUS is dedicated to creating a world where our relationship with animals is guided by compassion. We seek a truly humane society in which animals are respected for their intrinsic value, and where the human-animal bond is strong.

Want to help animals? We have plenty of suggestions. Adopt a pet from a local shelter, join The Humane Society and be a part of our work to help companion animals and wildlife. You will be funding our educational, legislative, investigative and outreach projects in the U.S. and across the globe.

Or perhaps you'd like to make a memorial donation in honor of a pet, friend or relative? You can through our Kindred Spirits program. And if you'd like to contribute in a more structured way, our Planned Giving Office has suggestions about estate planning, annuities, and even gifts of stock that avoid capital gains taxes.

Maybe you have land that you would like to preserve as a lasting habitat for wildlife. Our Wildlife Land Trust can help you. Perhaps the land you want to share is a backyard— that's enough. Our Urban Wildlife Sanctuary Program will show you how to create a habitat for your wild neighbors.

So you see, it's easy to help animals. And The HSUS is here to help.

THE HUMANE SOCIETY
OF THE UNITED STATES

2100 L Street NW • Washington, DC 20037 • 202-452-1100
www.hsus.org

TRADEMARK STATEMENT

DEDICATION

I would like to dedicate this book to my husband, Tom, for his unwavering support of all of my endeavors, and to my mother, who always believed in me. I miss her so much I can hardly breathe. And to my sister, Melissa, and my nephews, Wesley and Logan, because they inspire me. I love them all.

TABLE OF CONTENTS

Chapter 3: Doing Your Research   67

Chapter 4: Writing a Business Plan   75

Chapter 5: Buying a Franchised Interior Design Business   95

Chapter 6: Getting Started   105

Chapter 7: Internal Bookkeeping   119

Chapter 8: Budgeting & Operational Management   123

Chapter 10: So You Have a Sales Lead... Here is What You Do Next   153

Chapter 11: Congratulations! You Got the Project...Now What?   173

Chapter 12: Current Trends in Design 177

Chapter 13: Green Design 187

Chapter 14: Preparing to Leave Your Business 203

Conclusion 207

Appendix A: Interior Design Forms 209

Appendix B: Financial Forms   241

Appendix C: Case Studies   245

Glossary   265

Bibliography   277

CHAPTER 1

Interior Design 101

A Brief History of Interior Design

Designing our interior spaces can be traced back to the Roman Empire and ancient Greece. Since man has been building dwellings, we have been decorating those interior spaces. Primitive man may have been "decorating" their cave walls and their bowls and pottery, but as civilizations evolved throughout the world, so did design. We know about the Roman and Greek architecture and design from ruins, surviving furniture pieces, and a few literary sources that give us an insight into what ancient man was doing and thinking about their dwellings and design. We have much more to look at from the Roman ruins, but it is important to note that the Romans took much of their basic design elements from Ancient Greece and built upon them.

The Renaissance period gives us amazing insight into the importance of design in the ancient world. Italy and France were epicenters of design from the Renaissance and beyond. It was during the Baroque era, however, that domestic interior design began to emerge on its own, rather than as an afterthought of the architectural design.

Between the 1700s and 1800s, there was a decline in standards in the approach to interior design. Design was becoming more available to the masses. Early Modernism was an interesting time for design. At the turn of the century, Frank Lloyd Wright (1869-1959), studying under Louis Sullivan (1856-1924), was becoming one of America's predominant designers, presenting the concepts of large, open interior spaces, and this style remained an important influence in American design. Wright did not design based on the past historical designs, but to the desires and needs of his clients. He took an approach of integration.

Dorothy Draper

The first lady of interior design in America was Dorothy Draper. Born in 1889, Ms. Draper opened the first interior design business in 1923, when it was unheard of for a woman to open a business of any kind. Her style was modern, as she broke away from the "period room" styles of the time. She enjoyed designing public spaces, and many still exist to this day, such as her work with the restaurant at The Metropolitan Museum of Art® in New York.

Ms. Draper used vibrant colors and combinations, and one of her favorite combinations —and there are many famous ones — was dull white and glossy black. Her signature "cabbage rose" chintz fabric is still popular today. Ms. Draper wrote a design advice column for *Good Housekeeping*® magazine, designed custom fabrics and furniture, and decorated restaurants, theaters, department stores, hotels, and private homes. You can see some of her work at The Carlyle in New York and at the Greenbrier in West Virginia, where she designed a room called "The Victorian Writing Room," called one of the most photographed rooms in America. She was truly a pioneer of our modern design business.

Exploring Your Passion for Interior Design

Are you constantly redecorating your home? Do your friends and family ask you to help them redecorate rooms in their home? Do you watch HGTV® constantly and think, "I could do that?" These are just a few indicators that you might be a designer.

I suggest that you read about the different design styles and try to determine what your design style is. Do you like to create? Are you the type who sees potential in an old piece of furniture at a garage sale? Have you ever painted an antique piece of furniture? Do you have a creative flair? If you surf the Internet, you might consider signing up for some design blogs and reading them. There is so much involved in the actual talent of design that you will not get bored. Whether it is learning about furniture scale, how lighting in a room contributes to or takes away from the design of the room, or how paint colors interact with each other, read and study as much as you can. You might want to find designers whose style you identify with and study their work — you could work as a design assistant part-time for another designer or even as an intern to see the daily workings of what it takes to own your own design business.

If you have a definite favorite style of your own, will you be able to design a room for a client who wants the exact opposite of your style? Do you want to be considered a designer who only designs in your chosen style, or do you want to be a designer who works with clients' tastes and can offer whatever style they want? Often, a designer will start out designing for their clients' tastes, and as he or she becomes more known and successful, that particular style is recognized, and the people who want that style gravitate toward them and become their clients. At that point, the designer has enough of a following that he or she can specialize in their own specific design choice.

Photographs provided by Cindy Hernandez

A Current Market Overview

Employment is growing in this area, driven by U.S. households and small businesses. It is estimated that there will be a 4.5 percent growth rate for this industry through 2012. A large part of this market will come from hospitality, which includes restaurants, hotels, motels, and resorts that need someone to design or redesign already-existing establishments. Many tourism areas with hotels have to constantly remodel and reinvent their properties to keep tourists coming back. Corporate clients want to expand or improve their offices, or create new retail stores and leisure facilities for families.

As people work more from home and altogether stay home more often, home offices are a growing trend, as are home media rooms. Similarly, another trend is larger bathrooms with saunas, whirlpools, and large walk-in closets. The green design movement is also strong and will continue to grow.

Whether you need formal education to work in interior design depends on whether you work in contract or residential design and what state you live in. Residential design often does not require a formal degree, while contract design can be more limited. There are many successful residential designers who do not have any higher education, however; many work long hours and have good sales skills and an eye for design.

In most states, you will find many accredited interior design programs to choose from. The Foundation for Interior Design Research posts a list of accredited schools on its Web site at **www.accredit-id.org**. Depending on the size of the state, the number of accredited programs may vary. About 50 percent of designers practicing in the United States who have postsecondary education have two or more years of college, and another 40 percent have a four-year college degree in interior design. The remaining 10 percent have their degrees in fine arts, liberal arts, industrial design, or other majors. There are many designers who have an innate talent and ability and have taught themselves the art of decorating or have interned with someone.

Trends in Interior Design

- Eco-friendly design using natural products is quite popular. Clients can appreciate a designer who is able to present them with natural, sustainable products, such as bamboo flooring, cork wall covering or flooring, and many more options as this field continues to grow. Clients are savvy in this area and want products that help them conserve energy and protect the environment. More solar water heaters are being installed than ever before, and also popular are ovens that cut cooking time in half.

- Customized and spacious bathrooms are highly in-demand.

- Especially in warm-weather states, outdoor living spaces are designed in lush style, including outdoor kitchens and bars, outdoor living room furniture, and outdoor fabric drapery.

- Faux painting is still in-vogue in many areas, and wallpaper is making a strong comeback. The trend is strong in Europe and catching on in the states. The new wallpapers have designs with texture and depth, as well as easy-to-remove backings. Large geometric shapes and tone-on-tone patterns are also popular.

- Remodeling of kitchens into luxury kitchens is another strong trend. As other areas are slowing, the baby boomers are spending money on luxury kitchen re-designs that include state-of-the-art appliances, induction cooking, the latest hardware, and amazing cabinet designs.

Income Statistics

As the owner of an interior design business, a designer's salary and income will vary and is based on the type and amount of work they capture. You can earn anywhere from a minimal salary to quite a large one. The following numbers are based on designers employed by larger firms, but it gives a reference for small design-business owners.

In 2006, the median annual earnings for interior designers was $42,260. The middle group earned between $31,830 and $57,230. The lowest income was around $24,270, and the highest was about $78,760. Designers working for architectural or engineering firms make around $46,750, while those in specialized in design services earn a salary of around $43,250. Interior designers working for furniture stores earn an average of $38,989, and for building and supply dealers, the average is $36,350. Salaries often range widely, depending on the type of employer, experience, education, and reputation of the person. Your earnings potential is unlimited. As you gain more referrals and clients, you can charge more for your services, add design assistants, or add designers to your team.

Calculating Start-Up Money

The Small Business Administration offers some useful worksheets that you can use to help estimate the expense of starting your business. Not everything on the list will apply to your business; only worry about the items that do apply to your interior design business. The forms will be helpful to you in estimating how much financing you will need to get your business started. Estimating these costs based on a monthly expense will make it easier. This is not difficult, but it might take some time and leg work. It is a vital tool that you will use often. You may need to contact others to gather information to make your estimates.

BUSINESS STARTUP COSTS	
Salary of Owner/Manager (if applicable)	
All Other Salaries and Wages	
Mortgage/Property Taxes	
Advertising	
Delivery Expenses	
Supplies	
Telephone	
Utilities	
Insurance	
Taxes, Including Social Security	
Interest	
Delivery Cars	
Gas and Car Maintenance	
Maintenance (Facilities/Equipment)	
Legal and Other Professional Fees	
Dues/Subscriptions	
Leases (Equipment/Furniture/Etc.)	
Inventory Purchases	
Miscellaneous	
One-Time Start-Up Costs	
Fixtures/Equipment/Furniture	
Remodeling	
Installation of Fixtures/Equipment/Furniture	
Starting Inventory	
Deposits with Public Utilities	
Licenses and Permits	
Advertising and Promotion for Opening	
Accounts Receivable	
Cash Reserve/Operating Capital	
Other	
TOTAL	

* Your total amount will depend on how many months of preparation you want to allow before actually beginning operations.

Some thoughts on some of the expenses you will encounter during the start-up phase of your business:

- Expect additional costs after the initial setup is complete, and include them in your estimates.

- Many amounts may be prorated, including insurance, payroll, taxes, employee benefits, licensing fees, and marketing expenses.

- It is critical that you allow for enough cash for your initial purchases.

- The utility companies will normally require a deposit, so you want to include these expenses in your calculations.

- Obtain all required licenses and permits, including city and county occupational licenses and professional licenses. Even if you are working from a home design studio, most states require an occupational license.

- You must register with the state if you are a corporation or if you are using a fictitious name or a "Doing Business As" (DBA).

- Be sure to include opening marketing costs, which may include logo design, business cards, advertising brochures, mailers, ads, and signs.

- Depending on the type of business entity you decide to establish, you will need an attorney to draw up the documents that must be filed.

- Business insurance that you will want to consider includes business liability insurance, commercial auto insurance, disability insurance, health insurance, life insurance, and Workers' Compensation insurance.

- If you are purchasing a franchise, you will have additional fees, which will be discussed in more detail later.

- As you are a new business, many of your vendors will require prepayment for any orders until you have established credit.

- You should consider having a contingency fund that will keep your business going for the first six months. Many of your expenses will be higher in the initial start-up phase, and it is critical to have the fund for the unexpected.

Do You Have What It Takes to Be An Entrepreneur?

Once you have calculated the financial requirements for starting your business, you must decide whether you have what it takes to be an entrepreneur. Are you ready to work harder then you have ever worked? Are you ready to be responsible for every aspect of your business? Is your family supportive of your decision? Will they understand when you have to work a weekend or until 3 a.m. to finish a presentation? You need to realize that being a business owner is a full-time, seven-days-a-week job.

If you are still ready to move forward, the next step is make an honest assessment of your abilities and what you bring to the table for this business. Do you love to create? Are you good at dealing with people? Do you tend to have a positive attitude? Are you good with follow-up? If you determine you are not good at something like accounting, are you willing to pay an accountant to handle that part of the business for you, or will you insist on doing it all yourself? These are important questions, and they are just the beginning.

Traits of Good Entrepreneurs

Entrepreneurs are usually good with handling money. They know how to budget, get a good bargain when needed, and collect the fee from the client. Many started earning money as teens though babysitting, delivering newspapers, mowing lawns, raking leaves, shoveling snow, or even helping with cleaning.

Entrepreneurs are competitive. They typically enjoyed competing in school in team sports and achieving good grades to impress others and reach their goal. They might have excelled in track, soccer, or even writing; they had drive and were not afraid to be the best. They are not afraid to start their own business, work as a contractor, or try to sell a client on a design idea. They are good salespeople who are always thinking of new ways to make money and promote their services and ideas.

They are usually loners rather than joiners, often working as designers or consultants. They may work out of their homes because they can contact people via the Internet. They may often prefer a solitary work environment.

They often have good self-control, which means they are able to manage their time well and get the work done. They learn to temper their responses and do not overreact to situations that are stressful. They know how to spend down time and relax. They are realistic and will change their direction when they see the chance for success. They often verify the information they need before they use it.

They have the conceptual ability to analyze complex situations. They identify problems quickly and can begin working on them immediately. They are natural leaders who can find more than one way to solve problems.

Interpersonal relations refer to the skills a person needs to succeed in a business. Often, interior designers must have emotional stability and the ability to handle business pressures well. They should have the ability to work with others, delegate tasks, and, if necessary, work within a corporate structure. At the same time, they must have the ability to work independently and handle many details.

They think creatively and often do things differently than other people. They focus on continual learning, which means taking courses and seminars on their business or specialty.

Do You Have the Right Personality for the Job?

The following are some of the personality traits you need to become a successful designer. Look at the list and ask yourself whether you have the qualities needed to be a designer.

- Health is an important factor. Do you have good physical health to bend, carry samples, stretch, and work long hours? Long-term chronic health problems and serious medical conditions are often hindering to someone who wants to begin a business. Emotional health is another factor; you cannot become easily upset by setbacks and frustration. You need a positive attitude.

- You should be a self-starter who does not need someone to tell you what to do or to give you the initiative. This is an important trait because in your business, you will have to do many things that require independence.

- Enjoying people and being sociable is an important trait because you will be dealing with clients, vendors, architects, other designers, and even laborers. You must be able to get along and communicate with all types of people with different backgrounds and education levels.

- Leadership is important. You will be managing the entire project from beginning to installation. All involved in the project will look to you for leadership and direction on the project.

- Organization is critical. You will need to be organized and efficient with your time, managing many duties and responsibilities, such as client meetings, meeting with vendors, attending market, working on proposals, following the progress of jobs, and running the business end of your business.

- It is imperative to keep up with technology and trends in this field and to know your product.

- Good computer skills are important because many designers use computer software programs to design rooms, kitchens, homes, and offices. You will use the computer to order clients' materials, and keep records and other details of the business. You will likely also communicate with clients via e-mail.

- Good communication skills are important to get the job done. You must be able to talk with clients and vendors to get results. You must communicate with different people at different levels to solve different problems as they arise.

- Multitasking is the ability to do many different tasks at the same time, or the ability to juggle different projects to get results. You might be answering the phone, handling clients, and checking orders in the same hour.

- Presentation and sales ability are critical for success in your new business. If you hate sales, interior design is not for you.

- Confidence in your talent and abilities will help you in your success. Self-esteem and assurance in yourself will give your customers the confidence to work with you.

- The ability to deal with problems is crucial. Seldom will you have a project with no problems, as there are so many moving parts and so many people and companies that you must depend on to complete the project correctly. You will need patience, as the business will test you often. For example, an order might not come in on time, or the client might get the wrong stove delivered to the curb.

- Math skills are critical in this field because you will have to estimate costs to clients. You will need to write orders, collect money, and measure windows, doors, and cabinets for size and space to design them properly.

Look at the following Skill Assessment Inventory checklist and evaluate yourself and your talents. It is a place to start to determine whether you have what it takes to succeed in running your own successful interior design business.

SKILL ASSESSMENT INVENTORY		
Entrepreneur/Managerial Qualities	**Qualified**	**Not Qualified**
I am good at resolving conflicts		
I enjoy working hard		
I am able to meet deadlines		
I am able to maintain a budget		
I am a self-starter		
I am a creative problem-solver		
I set clear goals		

SKILL ASSESSMENT INVENTORY		
I have the ability to follow through		
Organizational Qualities		
I'm good with figures		
I keep an updated calendar		
I have to-do lists		
I have the ability to prioritize tasks		
I am good at recordkeeping		
I have a good filing system		
Communication Skills		
I am good at giving instructions/directions		
I am good at writing memos/letters/reports		
I am a good listener		
I speak clearly, making sure people understand		
Customer Service Skills		
I don't get frustrated easily		
I don't lose my temper easily		
I am comfortable with enforcing rules or policies		
I like to solve problems		
I tolerate all people, no matter their race gender or religion		
Hospitality Skills		
I am friendly and open		
I like working with people		
I enjoy pleasing people		
I enjoy helping people get the information they need		
I am optimistic		
I like to entertain		
I like to cook		
TOTALS		

CHAPTER 2

Are You a Designer?

E very state has its own licensing requirements regarding designers. Some states have licensing laws that may require a certain level of education and the passing of a state exam to be able to call yourself an "interior designer." Licensing gives only people who meet the state's criteria the right to call themselves interior designers, and there are a handful of states that have practice laws that tend to be very restrictive. There are many Interior Designers who may never have attended college at all who have been "grandfathered" in to licensing by states that now have licensing and practice laws on the books. As an interior designer, you will need to have professional membership with groups such as the American Society of Interior Designers® (ASID®) or the International Interior Design Association (IIDA).

What Interior Designers Do

Interior designers must know building codes, ADA requirements, fire codes, and permitting — these are all a few things that designers are responsible for that interior decorators are not, due to the more extensive nature of the projects that designers handle. Interior designers usually have a college degree in design and, in many states, they must pass a test by the

National Council for Interior Design Qualification (NCIDQ®) and usually must be a member of ASID.

Designers can do exactly what decorators do, but they can also do much more. For example, an Interior designer can offer architectural changes, do space planning, design built-in permanent furniture, and can provide reflective ceiling plans. They often work on commercial projects, such as hospitals, hotels, and resorts. Designers are responsible for knowing all codes that are created to protect the safety of the public. Because they often also offer the same services as the decorator, they will create a plan for a room, including furnishings, window coverings, flooring, wall coverings, and accessories — just like a decorator.

In some states, it can take up to six years of a combination of formal education, an internship under a licensed interior designer, and then passing the NCIDQ test before you can call yourself an interior designer and work on complete commercial projects.

A designer creates an interior space, whether it is the inside of a private home or the lobby of an office building. Designers meet with clients to gather information they need to work on a proposed design for the project. Often, especially when they own their own small design firm, designers handle the entire project, which includes the client meeting, the research for the right materials, the design of the space, the selection of the furnishings and fixtures, the design of the window coverings, the selection of the flooring and wall covering, paint selection, and even accessories. You will calculate pricing, order samples, place orders with vendors, and follow the progress while coordinating the installation and delivery to complete the project.

But you also should determine whether you prefer to work for a company where you have secure income and benefits without the responsibility of the business on your shoulders, or whether you are an entrepreneur and want to run your own show. If you are reading this book, you have likely determined that you want to own your own business.

A designer often helps a customer who cannot make any design choices for fear of making a mistake; to have a beautiful living space. They may offer special services, like weddings or holiday decorating. On the surface, this seems simple and fun, and with the era of HGTV, many people think they are designers. However, what you see on the show is basically the fun part — the end result. A designer does much more. As a designer, you will need the following:

- Creativity and talent
- Knowledge of decorating and design basics
- Specific education and licensing for work on commercial projects in certain states
- Salesmanship
- Mathematical aptitude
- Project management skills
- Artistic talents for sketching designs
- Ability to visualize the finished design

This is only the beginning, as you are also a small business owner and you are running the business end of your business, which involves tracking orders, accounting, sales, marketing, and, if you have employees, human resources. There is quite a bit of sales, paperwork, project management, and math involved in operating an interior design business. To run any successful business, you must also be prepared to work long hours.

Some designers choose to work from a home-based design studio and meet with their clients at the clients' homes, while others choose a retail space where they can bring their clients to their studios for presentations. Another option is to operate and work out of a retail store where they sell products *and* offer design services. Technology allows designers to work almost anywhere, and communicate and share information easily. The least expensive overhead is to work from a home studio and meet clients at their location. Additionally, it makes sense to show a customer fabrics and drawings in the actual room you are decorating. A retail store, or even a retail office studio, will incur more overhead and require more start-up capital, which we will discuss in later chapters.

There are usually two areas in the interior design world: residential and commercial. Within these two main areas, there are specialized fields, and some designers will specialize in specific niche areas of design. Specialization can lead to greater profits, especially if you focus on an area where there is less competition for clients. Some designers focus on offices, others on homes, retail businesses, restaurants, hospitality, hospitals, corporations, schools, spas, or one of many other niche areas. You do not have to specialize in one type of design, but you might find that you naturally become specialized in a particular type of design, based on what is in demand in your area.

What Design Assistants Do

Design assistants help designers decorate the inside of a home or business, including helping with decorating many different types of businesses and homes. They might assist with the entire design of an interior of a house, or one or two rooms, depending on what the client wants. Designers often decorate art galleries, bed-and-breakfasts, restaurants, hotels, and stores. It does not always have to be a solitary process, though: Assistants are important. Many designers will want their assistants to have some design education, learning about paints, furnishing, fabrics, lighting, flooring, and other materials. They often must have the ability to measure and order products for clients to improve their homes or businesses, and they often have to improve a client's home within a certain budget. Assistants interact with clients and deal with the client's emotions and dreams of creating a certain style for their home.

Assistants often make product selections such as hard window treatments, like mini blinds, vertical blinds, shutters, and shades. It means the window covering is hard or made from a material that is study or durable. Soft window treatments are draperies, valances, and swags. They are all measured differently, so the assistant should know how to measure for hard and soft window treatments.

Another aspect that an assistant often deals with is soft treatments like custom bedding, pillows, and cornices. They have to know color and fabrics to match the room that they are helping the client with, and they have to know how to measure and order products and price the order correctly.

Some tools that the assistant uses are drafting templates, color and style wheels, fabric and wall-covering estimation tools, and computer software. Assistants may help the interior designer choose color schemes, paint finishes, cabinet styles, and other features of a room. They do the research to help clients find the best products to decorate the interior of a room.

- Flooring: carpeting, wood, tile, and vinyl

- Wall coverings: wallpaper, painting, or faux painting

- Furniture: case goods, including hard items such as tables, chests, and buffets, and upholstery, such as that used for chairs, sofas, and loveseats

- Window coverings: both hard and soft

- Accessories of all kinds

- Custom bedding

Assistants often help the clients select blinds, furniture, colors, fabrics, rugs, and shades; order the products; and have them delivered and arranged. They often work with a client to ensure they meet the budget while still delivering a quality product. They transform rooms by laying out the furniture and other accessories in the rooms. They often select paint, wallpaper, and other accessories to make the walls more attractive.

Assistants may help with any room in a home. They decorate living and family rooms, kitchens, recreation rooms, dining rooms, master bedrooms, nurseries, bathrooms, sunrooms, and decks. Assistants must know how to use colors correctly and select furniture and accessories that enhance the room. In selecting furniture, they must know style and good quality.

Attending Markets

Interior designers attend markets. There are furniture markets, accessory markets, flooring markets, and more. The two large, established furniture markets are High Point, in High Point, North Carolina; and the World Market, in Las Vegas. They both offer a spring and fall market. Different regions of the country offer accessory markets, including Atlanta, Dallas, New York, and San Francisco, to name a few.

It is important to attend markets so that you are up-to-date on the latest trends in home design, as well as the latest products and vendors. Clients want to know that you are staying current with what is going on in the world of design. Attending markets is fun, educational, and exhausting. The duration is one to two weeks, where all the suppliers are in one place and their showrooms are staged to showcase their latest products and trends. You walk for days. Some designers purchase at market, especially if they carry inventory. Many furniture store buyers make their purchases at market, as they must carry a certain amount of inventory on their showroom floors to qualify for the account and the pricing with certain vendors. As an independent designer, you most often will attend to get in-person face time with your suppliers and their reps, and to keep up with current trends. It helps to make an appointment with your rep so that you are sure to have their undivided attention for a few moments. There are seminars on varying topics at all markets, so allow for some time to attend the seminars as well. You can learn installation techniques, how to put together a design board, how to read blueprints, and what the latest color trends are from seminars at market. Take advantage of them.

Different Design Specialties

Commercial Office Design: Almost all headquarters or corporate offices require some type of design work. A designer will develop workspaces that meet the new work environment conditions, ADA requirements, and state codes. In the commercial realm, you will often be involved in designing reception areas, offices and workspace, conference centers, recreation rooms, cafeterias, audiovisual centers, and auditoriums. Schools, libraries, malls, and other complexes need audiovisual centers and auditoriums with updated technology. Designers must stay current on the latest trends and products in acoustics and design to meet the complex needs of today's businesses.

Barrier-Free Design: The Americans with Disabilities Act (ADA) requires designers to make public and commercial buildings accessible to people using wheelchairs or walkers. Providing access to people with disabilities requires knowledgeable, skilled designers who can meet the demand for facilities that offer this type of access. Buildings and products must meet certain standards to pass inspection.

Bathroom Design: Modern bathrooms have become a big selling point in some homes. Some have whirlpool baths, saunas, and hot tubs. Modern bathrooms for shopping centers, malls, and restaurants require up-to-date technology and equipment that meet safety and sanitary standards. They have toilets that flush automatically, and sinks with faucets that turn on and off with sensors. Environmental concerns have generated new products and procedures for designers to learn.

Condominiums, Apartments, and Co-op Designs: With the housing market developing so many different types of houses and other forms of living space, the designer has a large market to work in. Some designers do apartment complexes, senior developments, and condos. Designer often work on computer rooms, recreation rooms, dining rooms, and other areas outside the basic living space.

Country Clubs: These faculties usually have residential and commercial features; they must meet fire and safety standards and be functional for the groups of people who meet there. Many facilities have swimming pools, golf courses, restaurants, tennis courts, gyms, bars, bathrooms, and other features. Many have large rooms for conventions and parties.

Design for Children: There are many opportunities to create environments for children — from their own rooms to areas that are used by parents regularly. Current research claims that the right environment can motivate and excite a child to learn and grow. Many of the spaces like doctor's offices, libraries, schools, and stores need a creative designer who knows the product and design needs of children. Children's art is creative, and design can offer a chance to think like a child and in new, innovative ways.

Energy Conversation and Ergonomic Design: The way people use energy is a big area for designers. Designing solar rooms or structures in old or new homes takes a knowledgeable, specialized designer. Ergonomic design takes into consideration the way people use things in their physical environment. It is based on the physical needs of the body and takes into consideration the human body, human sensory capacity, body functions, and emotional satisfaction. Ergonomic design is part of designing for people in any given situation. This type of design may be applied to the work environment to keep it interesting so workers are productive.

Senior Design: This is a growing area of design. The baby boomers are aging and want need-specific design, whether in their own homes or in senior living facilities. Special design is needed for their apartments, nursing homes, assisted living centers, and senior centers. There are retirement communities that combine the living services with cultural centers for entertainment. These boomers expect a designer to design for their healthy, active lifestyle.

Historic Preservation: This specialty requires an interest in history and research. What were the colors of wood or wallpaper used in homes in the late 17th century? What hardware is appropriate for doors and windows? Did the fireplace use brick or stone? Does the client want the building historically accurate? Often, the designer works with clients who want to preserve homes, but historic preservation extends to historical museums, restaurants, and other buildings. Technology helps designers determine original colors and find dates on buildings when necessary.

Hospital Design: Today, hospitals are complex design projects that require specialized designers. Some have international practices. Some designers specialize in designing emergency rooms, intensive care units, or gift shops. Hospitals are always changing to keep up with medical developments. Designers often work with system technology using a demanding set of guidelines. One of the newest models of hospital design is warm and inviting, with patient rooms that offer space for relatives that stay with the patient. The environment is not so cold and sterile and is designed to put the patient at ease and to accommodate family members.

Hospitality and Restaurant Design: The hospitality/hotel area can be quite lucrative and includes bed-and-breakfasts, hotels, and motels. Restaurants range from fast-food stands in malls to upscale establishments. Designers must know about food, safety, design, and many other areas. This broad area offers good opportunities for specialization.

Kitchen Design: The kitchen is often the selling point of a house or an important part of a restaurant. Designers who specialize in designing kitchens must know about appliances and new technology. Designers must know about new products and the dietary requirements of the kitchen's users. The National Kitchen and Bath Association created a curriculum that is used by many design schools. Often in restaurant kitchen design, you must know equipment and how to adapt it to the individual requirements of the facility. Kitchen specialists often work for equipment suppliers on projects for schools, country clubs, and commercial restaurants. When designing a kitchen for a private residence, designers must create with the user in mind, maximizing the space and designing cabinetry that works with clients' lifestyles.

Medical Center and Office Design: Medical centers, rehabilitation centers, and specialized offices have specific requirements that only a specialist could keep track of. The designer must know medical codes, safety rules, and how to install specialized equipment. Technology is a big part of medical facilities, so this knowledge is important, too. There are many specialized medical centers for cancer, heart, kidney, birthing, and other specialties. Medical offices of doctors require designers who know the equipment, traffic patterns, and storage needs of different types of doctors. The knowledge of color, design, technology, and medical equipment is required. Change is constant in this field, which makes it demanding but lucrative for designers.

Resort Design: Resorts are often connected to hotels or tourism areas where many people go to visit or attend a convention or event. They are popular in large cities and urban areas that bring in people for many different reasons. Some resorts focus on sports, gambling, or even camping. Designers must know about the equipment used, general principles of the hospitality industry, technology, safety, and trends. It is an interesting area to specialize in, and many designers focus on specific types of resorts.

Spa Design: There are many spas for skin, weight control, beauty treatments, facials, plastic surgery, massage, and cosmetics. It is a specialized area, so designers can work exclusively in this area because the demand is high. It requires knowledge of color, design, specialized equipment, and the products that spas use, in addition to safety regulations.

A Day in the Life of Three Different Types of Interior Designers

Kitchen Designer

8:30 a.m. The designer is in a business meeting. The builder calls to say he has spoken with a client about kitchen and foundation plans. The client wants the designer to call him to talk about lights for the kitchen. He wants to go over spec sheets and select the lighting. The designer decides to call him after lunch when she has more time.

9:30 a.m. The designer works on some CAD drawings of a kitchen proposal for a new client.

10:30 a.m. The designer goes online to look at a cabinet Web site to review material and specs, and selects a style and design to present to the client with the CAD drawings. The designer takes a quick break for lunch while she looks over design plans and reads some new catalogs to keep up with current trends on kitchen design.

1 a.m. The designer finally calls the builder about the client. She discusses the type of appliances and cabinets that he wants. He talks about the horizontal beams he has for the kitchen and mentions that the building inspector will eventually be examining the site for safety and design in code. They discuss the electrical needs of the kitchen switches, wiring, fixtures, and what the project will cost. She plans to visit the site in the next day or so to see how she can make the project run more smoothly.

2 p.m. A client stops by the office to discuss her kitchen. They look at different types of refrigerators. The client wants a built-into-the-wall stainless steel model with an icemaker because she and her husband entertain frequently. The designer discusses the layout of the kitchen for easy informal entertaining, which includes plenty of counter space and a center island.

The client wants roomy wood cabinets in a country style. That is a broad description, so they spend at least an hour looking at specs. The designer spends two hours with the client, browsing refrigerator and cabinet options.

4 p.m. Another client comes in to discuss his kitchen. He is interested in looking at stoves and talking about the types of kitchen cabinets and flooring he wants. She shows him different types of stoves. He likes the stainless steel gas models with glass tops and wants stainless steel cabinets and counters because he is a chef and likes to cook when not working. He wants a bar in the kitchen area, too. He has a large kitchen area to work with. They spend about one hour on his project.

5 p.m. The designer spends the next hour reviewing some of the projects she is working on. She looks through her e-mail, answers any urgent messages, and listens to her voicemail.

6 p.m. She leaves the office for the day to return tomorrow at about 8 a.m.

Commercial Interior Designer

8:30 a.m. The designer arrives at the office to look over e-mails, listen to voice messages, and check interoffice mail.

9:30 a.m. The designer attends a meeting about the construction of current projects, including the design of a medical office complex. The designer consults with the architect, answers design questions, and then listens to a status report on how the building is coming along. The designer talks about the building inspection and goes over the safety codes and regulations. The meeting lasts a few hours.

11 a.m. The designer returns calls to several clients whose projects are in progress. He reads e-mails and responds to the most urgent ones. He returns calls about supply orders and sets up some appointments to talk with clients and suppliers. He checks on an office furniture order for a dentist office. It appears the furniture may not arrive for the grand opening. The client will not be happy.

12 p.m. The designer goes out to lunch and gets a sandwich and coffee at a local restaurant.

1 to 3 p.m. He spends some time in a sample library reviewing products for clients he will meet with over the next few days. He goes over carpet samples for a medical office he is designing and reviews specs of office furniture for a law office client. The rugs must be well-made and durable, yet elegant for the law offices. The doctor's office wants special attention paid to durability because of the high traffic they get from clients.

3 to 4 p.m. The designer meets with staff members to talk about a law office project they have just undertaken. They talk about the project design, building codes, regulations, and the overall design of the project. Each person will work on one aspect of the project and then meet again next week.

4 to 6 p.m. He reviews several stacks of orders for clients and checks on their status by phone. He checks on carpet, office furniture, windows, doors, a water cooler, and even cafeteria tables for a small corporation. The designer reviews and returns some e-mails, cleans up, and goes home.

Private Home Interior Designer

8 a.m. The designer has an appointment with a new client at their home. She meets the client, tours the client's home, and listens to what the client would like done. She asks the client about her budget. The client decides she would like a proposal, so the decorator asks for a retainer to pull the proposal together. The designer's schedules the next appointment, where she will bring the client a full presentation for the re-design of the living room.

10 a.m. The designer arrives at the office and opens the file of a project. She checks the job reports and determines that she needs to make some phone calls to vendors to check on the status of the furniture and the drapery to ensure that they will be delivered on time for the installation date.

11 a.m. The designer has scheduled an hour to send out billing invoices for consulting services and completed projects, then works on paying vendor invoices.

12 p.m. The designer leaves for lunch, where she is meeting with a Realtor-friend to discuss the possibility of a referral to the Realtor's new clients that have just purchased a new home and need window treatments.

1:30 p.m. The designer works on a proposal due in two days. She looks at photos of the client's windows and rooms, creates sketches of the designs she will propose to the client, looks through several fabric books to find the right fabric for the design, and begins calculating the amount of fabric needed for each window. At that point, she will calculate the cost of the fabric, the cost of the labor to fabricate the treatments, the cost of the hardware, the cost of the installation, and her fee or markup on the job. Finally, she types everything into a presentation and pulls the catalog with the hardware, the fabric books with the fabric samples, and the sketches together to prepare for the appointment with the client.

4 p.m. She checks e-mail, returns phone calls, and orders some fabric swatch samples for a client who has changed her mind on the fabric for the windows in her dining room.

5 p.m. She leaves for the day.

What an interior designer does depends on the type of design he or she does. The field has many specialties. Below are some general duties that apply to most designers.

- You will meet with clients and determine what they need, what their design style is, and their budgets.

- You will need to be able to visualize how products will work in the design simply by seeing them in product catalogs and sample books. You will have to develop a professional presentation to sell your concept or idea.

- You will often need to sketch window covering designs for presentation to your clients and create room layouts to show your client how you envision the placement of furnishings and fixtures. You might work on CAD for computerized designs.

- You will need to understand how to measure and design window coverings.

- You will have to know design and how to sell your ideas no matter what type of design you specialize in. You may be responsible for mapping out a room on a computer system, taking measurements for cabinets or flooring, and sometimes even showing clients how equipment works.

- You will have to price each job with equipment and supplies and estimating materials needed for each product or component of the project. Depending on the project, these estimates can be complex and detailed.

- You will have to order materials from manufacturers using phone, fax, or e-mail. You will manage the design project from start to completion, including following orders from vendors and coordinating delivery and install.

- When you deal with the product, you will have to check for flaws, missing parts, and correct design and color.

- You will create invoices and collect deposits and balances on orders from clients. You will do the basic bookkeeping and recordkeeping for the business.

- You will have to arrange for the products and installers to arrive on time at the site. If you order supplies, you will have to follow-up by calling or going to the site and checking. Sometimes you will have to deliver the product yourself, but the manufacturers and vendors you work with can often handle this job.

- You will deal with salespeople who sell the items and services you may use.

- You will have to keep up with what is current and discontinued from your vendors. It is time-consuming but necessary.

- You will have to market your business and network to find new clients.

General Traits Required to be a Designer

Patience is necessary in the world of design and when working with clients. There are many opportunities along the way that can create problems that might be frustrating to your client. Your calm and patience in dealing with these obstacles will allow you to successfully complete the project. You must be organized due to the many details of the job and the various functions you will have to do. You need to be motivated to seek out clients and projects; you must have good listening skills to hear your clients and work with vendors; you should have a genuine interest in people and be able to deal with stress and crises. And, of course, that is all on top of the required design ability, including being savvy about color, scale, lighting, furnishings, measurements and estimation, sketching, math, and details — and having confidence in your talents.

Being able to read a client is important. Some people know what they want, but they just do not have the time or inclination to do it themselves, and they want to tell you exactly what they want and have you handle it. More often, people are frozen out of fear of making a design mistake and cannot make a decision. They want you, the expert, to be confident and take control by making the selections for them. Many people cannot pull a complete room together; it takes talent and ability. They may know their favorite colors and their favorite design style, but need you to take it from there.

In this industry, you must love people and want to help them. They are entrusting you with their money to create a warm, comfortable interior space that they call home, or, if it is a lobby of a corporate office, the design will communicate their brand to their customers. Yes, design is fun, and seeing the completed project and a happy customer is priceless, but from start to finish, there is quite a bit of work thrown in along with the creative part.

A Look at Some High-Profile Designers

Charles and Ray Eames

Charles Ormond Eames and Ray-Bernice Alexandra Kaiser met in 1940 at the Cranbrook Art Academy of Art in Bloomfield Hills, Michigan. They married the next year in 1941, and worked together for the rest of their lives designing furniture and following their philosophy of simple but elegant design.

The Eames wanted everyone to have access to furniture that was functional as well as beautiful, hence their motto "better living through better design". The Kwikset House, a do-it-yourself home, offered premade parts to people desiring an affordable yet modern home. The Eames' networked with the federal government and large company figures like Henry Ford to promote the idea of mass production in a postwar America that needed to be rebuilt.

The couple's work includes the Eames Lounge Chair, an iconic piece of office furniture produced by Herman Miller. The chair is a perfect example of their work with plywood molded into shape, rather than cut and affixed together. They even built their own home in 1949 in Los Angeles, which is now a U.S. National Historic Landmark. The couple also nurtured a love of photography and cinema, so the Eames captured much of their designs themselves.

The Library of Congress has more information about the Eames at **www. loc.gov/exhibits/eames**.

Barbara Barry

Barbara Barry comes from a family of artists, and describes herself as seeing "the world very much in terms of light, form, color, and texture". She attended the Academy of Art College in San Francisco, and is now internationally known and been awarded many times over for her glamorous yet fluid design style. She is known for her keen attention to detail and emphasis of the lines present between pieces of furniture that unite the room as a whole.

Barry is a Renaissance woman of design, and has many of her own lines of various products with companies like Ann Sacks, Boyd, Kravet Fabrics, and Bloomingdale's. An entire room can be created with Barbara Barry products. She has decorated the homes of many famous people, and has recently taken to designing public spaces such as Avon Spa in New York City. She also created Barbara Barry Home Fragrances, with scents specifically made for each room.

Visit her equally elegant Web site at **www.barbarabarry.com**.

Nate Berkus

You might know Nate Berkus from the *Oprah Winfrey Show*. He became famous after a show in 2001 where he redecorated a small room, and Oprah loved his work. He is now a regular guest on the show as well as contributing editor of *O Magazine*. He also has published a book of his own in 2005 through Hyperion called *Home Rules: Transform the Place You Live Into a Place You'll Love*. He also has a blog he occasionally contributes to on the Home Shopping Network Web site.

Berkus was only 24 years old when he started his design firm, Nate Berkus Associates, in 1995. He claims to have loved decorating since childhood, helping his mother and neighbors to re-arrange their furniture for fun. His style is described as "modern and natural", and he promotes the idea of reflecting your personality in your living space.

Visit Berkus' Web site at **www.nateberkus.com**.

Vern Yip

Vern Yip loves to work cultural finishes from his homeland of Japan into his design, especially silk. Yet Vern is sensitive to the varying budgets people have, and can show his viewers watching Deserving Design how to remake a space on a budget or with six figures. Yip originally planned to be a doctor, and even earned two degrees before changing his mind and pursuing design. While he did not stay on the path of saving lives, he still feels the need to help others, and focuses his show on inspiring people and their stories, such a an episode about a family that survived Hurricane Katrina.

Read some of Yip's great advice at **www.vernyip.com/index.html**.

Candace Olsen

Candace Olsen is a highly successful Canadian-born designer. She has been working as an interior designer for 15+ years. Candace has a successful design show, *Divine Design*, on HGTV, as well as her own line of furniture, wallpaper, rugs, and more. Online, Olsen gives a run-through of the steps she follows to prepare for a show. First, she makes a site visit where she gathers all the details she will need to create the design for the space. Next, she creates a client binder where she keeps all paperwork pertaining to the design — including sketches. From there, Olsen begins sketching designs, and this is where she forms her concepts for the project.

Next is going and finding the right fabrics and finishes, sometimes from her sample room, and often from vendors. Then she creates color renderings for the crew and goes back to the site where she goes over the plans so everyone is on the same page. The goal is a seamless job and show, but as Olsen mentions, that never happens. Such is the nature of the design world. Something will almost always go wrong during the process because there are so many moving parts, and you are in charge of it all. You must be able to handle the problems and go with the flow.

For more information on Olsen, visit **www.divinedesign.tv/master.asp**.

An In-Depth Look at a Whole House Re-Design

By giving you a look at what is involved in a whole house re-design, you will have a good idea of what is involved in being an interior designer.

You get a call from a customer because they want to re-design their home. You schedule an appointment to meet with the client and talk about the project. Be prepared to get as much information as possible about the project and the client's wants, needs, and budget.

Here are some of the questions you might ask:

- Are you doing any structural remodeling?
- If so, do you have a contractor lined up?
- What budget have you established for the re-design?
- Are there any items or areas that you want to keep, or do you want a total makeover?
- Is there a specific style that you like?
- Do you have blueprints of the home?

As you ask these questions, you will receive many more questions. The goal is to get as much information as possible. The clients may have already decided on "the look" they want to achieve, or perhaps do not want to change the flooring, or they have specific ideas on flooring or other areas. If there are no blueprints to work off, get measurements of each room and take photos.

Decide on an overall look and feel of the home and try to strive to achieve it in every area. Ask the clients enough questions to know how they use each room, what they love, and what kind of lifestyle they lead so that you will know whether they want a formal or casual home. They may have favorite styles, colors, or strong opinions on what they want. Often, they will be looking to you for guidance in all these areas.

You will decide on an overall look based on the information gathered from the homeowner and the actual structure — or bones — of the home. You will look at flooring. Some people feel strongly about having carpet in the bedrooms and are open to wood flooring, tile, or stone in other areas. Which flooring works best for the home and the design? To soften wood flooring, tile, and stone, area rugs can add warmth, along with texture and color.

Selecting flooring samples is a good place to start. You might look at paint or wall treatments next, whose options include straight painting, wallpaper, fabric covering, and faux painting, to name a few. If a client wants the feel of an Italian villa, you might have tumbled stone floors with area rugs and Venetian plaster on some of the walls. Find a flooring vendor whom you are comfortable working with. There are membership companies open to the trade only, such as ProSource®, which specializes in flooring. If you join, you can bring clients into the showroom or take out samples to take to the clients' homes. The vendor gives you a discount, and you choose to keep the entire discount or pass along some of the savings to your client. Whether you are selecting wood, stone, tile, or carpet, there will be many things to consider about each type of flooring, including price, quality, size, and color. You will need to measure each room for flooring so you can calculate the price. Do not forget to include the installation and removal of existing flooring.

Wallpaper can be used on all the walls in a room or as an accent wall for a punch of color and design. After you find wallpaper samples that you want to show the client, order memo samples of the papers so you are not carrying big, awkward wallpaper sample books. Do not forget to measure the walls and calculate how much wallpaper you will need. Include in your price removal of existing paper or prepping the existing walls and installation.

Also take into consideration the paint on walls, which can set the mood for an individual room. The light coming into the room can help you decide the best paint colors. Paint chips are fine for examples, but you might want to get samples of the paint and paint it on wallboard or actually on the wall in the home in different areas so that you and the client can see what the paint looks like in the room at different times of the day. Does it look great in the morning light, but dark in the evening? Do not be afraid to paint the ceilings when appropriate for the design. Most painters will want to see the space to give you a price for painting. They are looking for obstacles, like how high the ceilings are, because they will need scaffolding if the ceilings are super high, and they will need to include that cost in their estimate.

Fabric-covered walls can be amazing, and the process is rather unique. You first place batting on the wall, then the fabric. There will be seams, as most fabric is 54 inches wide, but the seams can be covered with ribbon, contrasting fabric, or trim to add to the style. You will need wall measurements to calculate materials, and you will need an installer.

Next, you might look at window treatments. Does it make sense to have hard window treatments, such as shutters or wood blinds, alone on the windows? Or will you combine hard treatments with soft treatments, including drapery panels and a valance? Will your customer benefit from motorization of the treatments? Perhaps you will only use soft treatments, which can also include Roman shades or solar shades. You will need accurate measurements of each window so that you can design the treatment and price it correctly. Either you or your installer should measure at this stage. You might want to have the installer do a final measurement once all is approved and before you place orders to prevent costly errors. Do not forget materials, labor, freight, hardware, and installation in your estimate.

Designing window treatments can take quite a bit of time. You need inspiration to execute the planning, using a computer program or sketching the design by hand. Next, you select the fabrics and trims that you want in the treatment. You begin the work of confirming that all elements are available, not on backorder or discontinued, and you start pricing the treatments.

You will need to consider the layout and design of the kitchen and select new cabinets, or refinish existing cabinets — based on budget — as well as appliances and lighting. The client might want a completely contemporary

design, or perhaps a more traditional look. A popular trend includes kitch-
en cabinets that look like furniture and paneled appliances. There is an
increase in spending in luxury kitchen renovations, as people are deciding
to stay in the homes they are in and but still desire an updated kitchen that
fits their lifestyle. Countertop options might include granite, tile, Corian,
stone, or stainless steel. Stainless steel appliances and brushed nickel have
been in style for a while but show no signs of slowing down. You will need
to select water fixture shapes and materials as well; a relatively new trend in
this area is antique bronze. Having a showroom to take a client to can be
helpful if they are not sure what they like because they can touch and feel
the appliances and fixtures, and you can find the items they want and have
a good idea of what direction to go in based on their feedback.

There are also many decisions to keep in mind for remodeling the bathrooms. Features to consider include Jacuzzi tubs, larger showers, shower
heads, jets, fixtures, tile design for showers and tubs, toilets, sinks, mirrors,
flooring, and lighting.

With furniture, accessories, and lighting, take it room by room. What is
being kept that you have to work into the new design? What furniture is
needed for the room, and what furniture makes sense for the client's life
style? Is it a beach house? Do they need an office with a workable desk
area? Will there be a media room? If so, what wiring is needed, and do they
want a true theater-style room or a comfy sectional? How will you control
lighting coming in from the outside? What lighting is needed? Consider
overhead lighting and items like torchieres or lamps that will contribute to
the lighting design for each room.

Whether you use AutoCAD® or some other layout software, or you sketch
it by hand, you will need to give the client a layout of the furniture placement in each room. For a project of this size, you might want to have

sections to your proposal — such as window coverings, furnishings, painting, light fixtures, kitchen, and bathrooms — or you might want to give a proposal for each room. You will also want to create presentation boards and have samples to give the client the visuals they need to understand and get excited about the project.

There are always changes. Once you receive approval on the project, if you are working on a retainer, get that and get deposits. As the next phase of work begins, you will want to determine a timeline and what needs to be done in what order. You will coordinate every step of the re-design. I strongly recommend that you place orders with purchase orders (POs) and keep track of them — this is called "trafficking" projects. You might simply keep a copy of each estimate and PO together and note the date you placed the order, the date you expect to receive the items, and a date to follow-up on the order, or you could create a simple spreadsheet on Excel software and track the different parts of the order.

A Step-by-Step Guide to Designing a Bedroom

Your client wants you to design or re-design their bedroom. Clients are sometimes quite specific about what they want, and at other times, they might be completely overwhelmed at the thought of designing an empty room or re-designing an existing room. They look to you for guidance.

The place to begin is to interview your client. You have to know what purpose the room will be expected to serve. Yes, they will sleep in the room, but what else will they do in the room? Will they need a desk in the room? Will they want a reading corner? Are her needs different than his needs? You need to know the details so that you can successfully create a relaxing, welcoming space. Always interview the person or people who will be using the space; make sure you know the little details.

Step One: The client interview

You need to determine the following from the interview with your clients about the use of this space:

- Do they want a retreat, an escape, or a bright and cheery space?

- Do they sleep in?

- Do they watch TV in bed?

- Will they read in bed?

- Will the room serve double duty, with an office space in it?

- Do they want a space to read or meditate?

- Are you working with a blank slate, an empty room, or are you working around or with existing pieces of furniture?

- Does your client know what style they want — traditional, modern, spa-like, or romantic?

- Do they have a budget, and is it realistic for what they want you to do?

- Are there specific colors the client wants to work with, or perhaps existing window coverings or bedding that you will pull color and style from?

Step Two: Take measurements

Take measurements of the space, including the windows.

Step Three: Plan the design

Whether you will begin by selecting a paint color for the walls, a fabric for the window treatment, or the bedding is a personal decision. Use the method that works for you. Rissi Cherie, Interior Decorator and Window Fashions Certified Expert from Gainesville, Florida, says, "After establishing the style and atmosphere, we select the colors for the walls and fabric that will enhance the room the best." Rissi works with her clients to select wall and fabric colors first, which is a good path to follow. Your clients may ask that you build the design around a piece of furniture, existing bedding, or a certain fabric, so this is where you determine what they want. If they want a spa-like feel, you might look at warm, chocolate-brown furnishings with sea blues and greens in your fabrics. If they want a romantic, over-the-top design, this will lead you in an entirely different direction. This is the time to vet their desires and expectations for this space.

Window Coverings

The window coverings are crucial to the overall design of the room. For some clients, it is important to achieve complete privacy in the bedroom. Other clients might want to keep it light and bright. Begin by studying the window or windows and the surrounding wall. You might want layers on the window.

The first layer might include 2" wooden blinds, a Silhouette shade, a honeycomb shade, or perhaps a Roman shade. This layer will allow the client to adjust the amount of light that can come into the room. If the window is small in scale and you want it to look larger, you can add drapery panels on either side of the window. You can make the panels wide and bring them off the window onto the wall on either side, which will make the window appear larger.

If the ceiling is high, you might want to bring the drapery panels to the ceiling so that you do not break up the room with a horizontal line. If the window is short, bringing the panels to the top of the wall might elongate the window. If you stop with the two layers, you will want to select the best hardware. If the panels are more stationary, you might want a beautiful wood or iron rod with fabulous finials. If the panels are to be more functional, you can use a straight traverse rod, or you might use a decorative wood traverse rod. Brushed nickel hardware on the market can help finish a modern look. If you are not adding a top treatment, what will the top of your drapery panels look like? There are many options to choose from. Because it will be visible, choose one that reflects the overall look you are going for in the space.

If the style fits, you might add a top treatment. A formal style might include swags and jabots, while a more modern look might include a box-pleat valance. A romantic look would look good with a puffy, wrapped scarf. There are many standard styles of valances and top treatments, and you can get creative and make the top treatment fit the exact space you are designing by adding a special twist on how you use the fabric, or adding unique embellishments or beautiful trim.

Think about how trim might enhance the look of the treatment. Beautiful trim can make the window treatment or finish the look. Perhaps you use a basic fabric and go all out on the trim, or you have a gorgeous fabric, and a simple but elegant trim finishes the look. The popular trim colors lately are chocolate with gold, bronze and brick, and dark, earthy tones.

Next, it is time to determine what furnishings you need and what the space will accommodate. You want a bedroom to feel inviting and uncluttered, so you do not want too much furniture in the space. However, you always need to meet the client's needs.

Bed

Will the space hold a king bed, or will putting a queen bed in the space allow you to accomplish all of the client's requests for the space? The mattress is an extremely personal selection, and you might consider asking the client to go to a mattress store, either alone or with you, to select the mattress that will meet their needs.

Nightstands, Dressers, and Chests

Will the space allow for two nightstands? If you have the space, you can use a bachelor chest as a night stand on one side of the bed and a regular nightstand on the other side.

All factors are dependent on client needs, space availability, and the look or style. Will you have a wall that will be a perfect fit for the dresser, or will you need a chest on one wall and a lingerie chest on another?

Armoire or TV Stand?

If clients watch TV in bed, you will want an armoire or TV stand. If they want to be able to hide the TV, an armoire is the perfect solution; however, if they want the flat-screen TV to be part of the look and feel of the space, a clean-lined TV stand might be a better choice.

Upholstery Pieces

Will your space allow for a seating area? One or two upholstered chairs with an accent table, or perhaps a chaise or small sofa and ottoman, make a nice sitting area for reading and meditating. Custom-selected fabrics will add to the overall look of the room. Select pieces that are smaller and will not be oversized and make the room visually cluttered.

Lighting

Do you need to allow for lighting that will give enough light for reading in bed? Do you need overhead lighting, or just accent lighting? Lighting will affect the paint colors you select for the room.

Bedding

Based on the look and the client's budget, what will the bedding look like? You will want to measure the bed that the bedding will go on. Do not rely on general measurements because each type of mattress on each frame can be a different measurement.

Bed Cover

Is the bed a four-post bed? Will you use a crown or panels on the four-post bed?

If you do not have posts, you want to determine what type of comforter you will use. Will it be a bedspread, coverlet, or a duvet? Will it be ruffled, box-pleated, or is it a spread that you want to add scalloped fringe or a welt to? The whole look and feel of a bedroom can be changed by simply changing the duvet cover.

Dust Ruffle/Bed Skirt

Often the bed frame is meant to be seen, and you can either add a dust ruffle or bed skirt and tuck it behind the frame or not use one at all. If the bed begs for a skirt to complete the look, you must decide the best look for the entire bedding ensemble. Will you use a tailored skirt, a shirred skirt, or perhaps a box-pleated ruffle?

Headboard

Does the frame of the bed have a gorgeous headboard, or are you creating a modern, clean-lined room or romantic space where you might want to add an upholstered headboard? There are various shapes you can use for the headboard. Upholstered headboards are back in style. A custom upholstered headboard can help set the tone.

Pillows and Shams

You will want to decide on the style of the shams and whether they will have trim. Decorative pillows can complete the bed nicely. An odd number of pillows tends to work best. Bolsters add interest, and you can do fun custom pillows here.

Accessories

Accessories become the final touch, and you do not want to add too many and clutter the space, but just enough to finish the space. Are you using original art, abstract prints, or perhaps word art for the walls? It all depends on the look and the space.

Walls

Are you going to paint the walls a light color that will make the room look more spacious? Or perhaps the design of the space calls for a deeper color that will make the room warm and inviting. You might want to use faux painting for an accent wall, or perhaps wallpaper or fabric on the walls will finish the look.

Flooring

You might be working with existing flooring, or perhaps the client's budget allows you to change the flooring. A wood floor is warmed up with a nice area rug; an area rug on top of a neutral carpet works well, also. If the floor color is kept neutral, it will allow for whatever fabrics you select for the room, and you can use that beautiful area rug to add additional pattern, texture, and color.

Present the design

Take all the measurements you need to work with and start creating your design by selecting the furnishings, lighting, accessories, bedding, and window treatments for the space.

When you return to meet with your client and you show him or her the colors, fabrics, window treatment designs, and furnishings, the client will feel confident that you can pull this together. As you show what you have selected, talk about why you selected this particular fabric or chair. Explain why the window treatment design you created works for the room and the window. Refer to what the customer told you he or she wanted. Giving clients as much information as possible about how you arrived at your selections will help them feel confident in your design.

Take it step by step, and you will have a successful bedroom design — and a happy client.

PANEL TOP IDEAS	
Grommets	Pleats
• Knobs or Pegs can be used to"hang" the panels on the wall	• Fan-Pleat • Pencil-Pleat • Box-Pleat • Goblet-Pleat • Cartridge-Pleat • Triple-Pleat • French-Pleat
Tabs	
Clips	
Ties	
Looped	Rod Pocket
Smoked Heading	Gathered Header

MEASURING FOR BEDDING	
It is ideal to measure with existing bedding — such as sheets and blankets — installed.	
Width	Measure from the left side to the right side of the mattress — top only.
Length	Measure from the top of the bed at the headboard to the foot of mattress — top only.
Drop	Measure from the top edge of the mattress to where you want the bottom of the comforter or duvet to hang.
Dust Ruffle	Measure the Dust Ruffle.
Width	Measure from the left side to the right side of the box spring — top only.
Length	Measure from the top to the foot of the box spring.
Drop	Measure from the top edge of the box spring to where you want the hem of the dust ruffle to hang; allow ½" – 1" clearance at the floor so the ruffle does not drag.

CHAPTER 3

Doing Your Research

Buying an Existing Business or Starting Your Own

You have three options as you begin this journey. You can start your business from the ground up; purchase an existing private business; or purchase a franchised business. Whatever your decision, you will need to do the proper market research. The following information will be critical if you decide to purchase an existing business.

Finding the Best Location

The first step is to be prepared to deal and to know what you are looking for. Consider the following:

- Have an idea of the price you are willing to pay.

- Determine the terms you are willing to agree on for a purchase.

- Educate yourself so that you will be able to analyze the potential seller's sales price.

- The reality is that you will be working long hours and spending considerable time in this location, so you want to make sure you will feel safe, comfortable, and inspired here.

Next, make a list of things you must have and items that you are willing to trade or give up. A successful deal includes give and take. Consider the following factors:

- **Getting the best price**: Do not have an emotional attachment when considering the sales price. Instead, be certain that you do not pay more than then you are willing to pay, or more than the business is worth.

- **Making a down payment**: An acceptable down payment of 20 to 30 percent will be expected. If you put more than that down, you may run the risk of using too much of your available money on a down payment and causing financial restraints in your business.

- **Limiting your chance of failure**: Statistics show that 20 percent of purchased businesses fail, while 80 percent of new businesses fail. The quality of the business you are purchasing will contribute to your success.

From there, it is important to do your due diligence and find out about the reasons the seller is selling the business.

- **Retirement**: Some people want to sell the business and build up their retirement fund.

- **Disillusioned owners**: If an owner has been an absentee owner, and the business has started to decline due to their absence, or if they had a star employee running the business that has left, they may want to get out when they cannot find a qualified manager.

- **Tax problems**: Are all taxes current, or are there taxes owed? Perhaps the owner has maximized all the tax benefits and is choosing to sell and reinvest in another business.

- **Other opportunities**: Perhaps the owner may have other investment possibilities and needs to sell the business to generate income to fund their new venture.

- **Distressed owners**: The owner may have personal difficulties, including failing health or family situations. Perhaps a partner has left and made it difficult to continue the business.

Population and Demographics

One of the best places to obtain details about the population and demographics about a particular area in the United States is the U.S. Census Bureau (**www.census.gov**).

Consider the following demographics for evaluation:

- Population density
- Age groups
- Employment statistics
- Personal and household income

Another good source of information is the local Chamber of Commerce. The chamber can help you determine economic and life style patterns of the community. Other places to look for information would be your public library and online sources.

For additional information, visit the following online sites:

- **www.prb.org**
- **http://quickfacts.census.gov/qfd/index.html**
- **www.melissadata.com/Lookups/index.htm**
- **www.census.gov/acs/www/**
- **http://censtats.census.gov/**
- **http://factfinder.census.gov**

The American Community Survey: This is additional information from the supplemental census survey. It provides full demographic information for communities each year, not just every ten years.

Censtats: This Web site provides economic and demographic information that allows you to compare by county. This information is updated every two years.

The Small Business Administration

The Small Business Administration Web site, at **www.sba.gov/smallbusinessplanner/index.html**, has a wealth of information for starting a small business. It gives you four areas of information:

1. Planning your business
2. Starting your business
3. Managing your business
4. Getting out

Competition

You should search out your competition, which could be other design and decorating firms, both large and small; retail furniture stores; retail window-covering companies; and any stores that are selling accessories, wallpaper, and flooring. If they are retail operations, shop them. Ask for pricing. Also use the following as sources of more information about competition:

- **Telephone books, print and online**: Look in the yellow pages' book or Web site (**www.yellowpages.com**) under headings including "Interior Designers," "Interior Decorators," "Window Treatments," "Furnishings," and "Flooring." Gather the phone number and location of your competitors.

- **Chamber of Commerce**: The Chamber will have lists of local businesses.

- **Local newspapers**: Study the local paper for advertisements from competitors.

- **Internet**: Do a search for top keywords in your area, and take note of your competition and their Web addresses.

It can be a challenge to gain personal information on your competition in the design industry. You could ask a friend to shop some of them; however, some charge for the initial meeting.

Valuing Other Assets if Purchasing a Business

You will want to get a good idea of what is included if you are purchasing an existing business. It usually includes furniture, fixtures, equipment, supplies, and customer mailing lists. Keep in mind that positive name recognition is an important consideration in the value of a business.

The following are some factors to consider in determining a realistic sale price:

- **Profitability**: This is crucial. Check out the books and look at the profit margins.

- **Existing Lease Terms and Conditions**: Is there a lease? What is the amount of time left on the lease? What are the terms, and what are the monthly payments?

- **Franchise Affiliation**: If you are purchasing a decorating firm that is part of a franchise, you will also be paying a fee to the franchisor and might be required to be approved by the franchisor in order for the sale to occur.

- **Terms**: These are the details of how the buyer will pay the seller.

Review the Books

When considering the purchase of an existing business, you will want to review the books. You can hire an accountant to do it, and he or she can tell you whether they look sound. You or the accountant will need to analyze the balance sheet and income statements. You can learn quite a bit about the current owner's management skills from the balance sheet.

The Small Business Development Centers (SBDC) offer free consulting services to small businesses with less than 500 employees. You can also contact your local SCORE chapter. SCORE comprises retired business people who consult with and help small business owners for no charge. Their Web site is **www.score.org**.

Financing

The Small Business Administration (SBA) can be a source of loans for new small businesses. The SBA specializes in two types of loans. One, known as

Flagship 7, is a program primarily used for working capital for businesses. The Certified Development Company program is also known as the 504 Loans. It is used for buying or remodeling land, buildings, machinery, and equipment. Women received more than 25,587 SBA loans in 2005, and a grand total of $3.4 billion was loaned to people nationwide. This represented a 39-percent increase in the number of loans.

There are several advantages to using a SBA loan for your interior design business: You have longer repayment terms of seven to ten years. Some real estate loans, if you purchase a building or land for an interior design business, are extended to 25 years or more. Collateral is not required, but must be pledged to the SBA if you have it. Banks are more willing to finance risky ventures with these loans for small businesses. The disadvantages include slightly higher interest rates, and sometimes the rates can go up. There might be additional requirements that have hidden fees, which often add up, and the approval rate for the loan takes longer than some loans that take only a day for approval. You have to wait longer, and if you buy an established design company or franchise, you may find it easier to finance.

With SBA loans, the funds are available to any small business owner, and the SBA studies how successful the businesses are that get funding. It offers financial management and technical assistance programs. Check with your local SBA for information about loans and grants for your business.

Many new business owners use unconventional means of financing their startup. Often, owners will use personal credit cards and credit lines to start their businesses, or will look to family and friends to borrow money for their start-up ventures. Of course, this can be a tricky way to go. If the business fails, you may create problems with a family member or a friend. You will want to sign a formal contract or agreement with an interest rate, dates of payback, and other details.

A final consideration that many look to is to take equity out of their homes. Of course, this puts your home on the line. These unconventional ways of financing your business are not to be considered lightly. There are potential downsides to them, and you must weigh the risks against the benefits of using them.

Banks and credit unions are cautious when dealing with a small business or a start-up business, and they will want plenty of information. In addition to a solid business proposal and a detailed business plan, they will need to see how you intend to repay the loan. This might include several income sources, including:

- Enough collateral to secure the loan
- A signature loan with a good credit score
- A co-signer
- Equity in real estate you own that could be used as collateral
- Your assets-to-debt ratio, if applicable
- Whether you have a savings account, stocks, bonds, or other investments
- Cash value on a life insurance policy

CHAPTER 4

Writing a Business Plan

If you want to have a successful business, start with a business plan. Do not be intimidated. This investment of time and thought will be one of the best investments you will make for the success of your business. If you are asking for an investment or loan, you must have a good business plan, but even if you are financing the start-up of your business yourself, a business plan gives you a blueprint to follow. Review it frequently, and adapt and revise it when needed. If you need further assistance, talk to the SBDC nearest you. They offer low-cost seminars on how to write a business plan and usually provide free counseling and assistance. You may also consider contacting SCORE.

Just a few of the powerful benefits of having a well thought-out business include:

- Clearly defined ideas and goals for your business
- A succinct mission statement
- A blueprint to follow to help you stay focused on your goals
- A realistic view of what you are facing
- Realistic information to help you decide whether you will need financing to get the business going
- A realistic assessment of what type of profit your business can make

Keys to Success

Do your research. Study the area you will work in or locate your business in. Is there a niche that needs to be filled? The following "keys to success" research will contribute to the chances of success with your business.

- Is it in an area with new communities and subdivisions, with new homeowners who will need your services?

- Is it in an older, wealthier area that regularly uses interior designers?

- Is there a specific interior design niche that is not being served? Can you offer those services and fill that void?

- Will the area provide enough potential customers who choose to work with a designer?

- What is the competition? Are there too many designers in the area? If there are no designers in the area, figure out why this is.

- What is your target audience? Does this area provide potential clients who can afford your services?

- Is your pricing realistic for the area?

- Will you have a home studio and meet with clients in their homes, or will you have a retail store or studio?

- If you will have a retail store or studio, have you chosen a location that is convenient and accessible for your clients?

- Find out what the potential clients in that area want. Do they want consultation, custom window coverings, and custom furniture?

Are they renovating and re-designing existing homes and rooms, or are they building new homes?

• What will you do to stand out from the competition? Study the competition; their services, marketing, and advertising; and their customer service. What can you do to stand out from the crowd and create top-of-mind awareness?

The previous success keys are just the beginning of your research. To have a comprehensive, well-written business plan, you will need to do sufficient research. Research can be fun and interesting, and often, what you find will surprise you. The research will be invaluable in establishing credibility with lenders and investors.

The Four Main Sections of a Business Plan

A business plan consists of four main sections:

1. A description of your business.
2. An outline of how you plan to market your business.
3. Your management plan.
4. An outline of your financial management plan.

You will fill in the details in each section from your research. You will also add an executive summary, any documentation that will support your conclusions, and your financial projections for your design business.

Contents of Your Business Plan

The following list can be used to create your business plan outline. You will want to review the plan often during your first year, as there will inevitably be changes and updates to your plan. Update and change the plan to reflect the removal of ideas that did not work, or the addition of new ideas or expanded ideas that will assist you in more successfully targeting your customers.

Elements of a Business Plan

- Cover sheet

- Statement of purpose

- Table of contents

- Description of business

- Marketing

- Competition

- Operating procedures

- Personnel

- Business insurance

- Financial data

- Loan applications (if applicable)

- Balance sheet

- Break-even analysis

- Capital, equipment, and supply list

- Three-year summary/projection

- Detail by month, first year

- Pro-forma cash flow

- Pro-forma income projections (profit and loss statement)

- Detail by quarters, second, and third years

- Details about the assumption upon which your projections were based

- Tax returns of principals for the last three years

- Personal financial statement — your bank will have a standard form

- If you are buying a franchise, a copy of the franchise contract and all supporting documents provided by the franchisor

- Copy of proposed lease or purchase agreement for building space, if applicable, or explanation about having a home studio

- Copy of licenses and other legal documents

- Copies of résumés of all principals

- Copies of letters of intent from suppliers

Business Plan — A Description of the Interior Design Business

Start by asking yourself what type of design business you want to start. You have done the research; you know the niche(s) that need to be filled, so in the description portion of the business plan, you should give a detailed description of your business. Make sure you include in this statement your products, your services, the market, and a comprehensive description of the things that make your design business stand out from the crowd. Try to be flexible, and modify this statement as needed.

The first section is a description of your business; Section 2 describes your products and services; and Section 3 provides an explanation of your business location and why this location is the best spot for your business. With these statements, you will clearly identify your goals and objectives, which will explain why you want to be in business.

Your business description should include:

- Your business name and positioning statement or tag line

- Your business structure — whether you will be a sole proprietorship, partnership, or corporation

- Details on what licenses or permits are needed

- A succinct description of your business or what you do in about 25 words or 30 seconds. This can then become your 30-second commercial. It is common to devise a 30-second commercial for networking and for telling potential clients what you do quickly.

- An explanation of your products and services. What will you offer your clients?

- Whether you will purchase an existing design business or franchise, or whether you will be a new start-up design firm

- What your expectations are for profit and what your expansion plans are for the future

- Any information you have learned from your contact with suppliers, bankers, vendors, other franchise owners, or the franchisor, or any other research

- A cover sheet before the first page that includes all your contact information

Legal Business Forms

You will have to choose which business structure will best fit your needs. One element that will help you in your choice is whether you will be the sole owner or will have partners. Another large consideration will be tax and legal benefits that apply to various types of businesses. We will go over differences in this chapter. Review more details on each structure on the accompanying CD-ROM. Consider discussing the options with your attorney and accountant. They will provide you with the advantages and disadvantages of each. The tax and legal ramifications of each structure will impact the decisions made in your business.

The following are brief descriptions of each of the business structures to consider:

- **Sole Proprietorship**: By far, this is the easiest, least expensive way of starting a business. You can start a sole-proprietorship business by simply finding a location and opening for business. Your attorney's fees are typically less than the other business forms. You as the sole owner will have complete authority to make all business decisions. The risk or potential downside to being a sole proprietor is that you are personally liable if the business defaults on a loan or is involved in a legal dispute. If a client sues you, your personal assets are exposed.

- **Partnership**: This business structure is applicable when two or more people share ownership of the business. The two most common partnership types are general and limited. The general partnership requires only a verbal agreement between the involved partners, but it is strongly recommended that you have a signed partnership agreement. You will incur legal fees from an attorney to draw up the contract, but the costs are less than the cost of incorporating. Having a written agreement will help resolve disputes. With a partnership, all the partners are held responsible for each partner's actions. Therefore, if the business is sued, all partners are held liable.

- **Corporation**: A corporation has stockholders. There are different types of corporations and, therefore, you might want to consult with your attorney about which type of corporation structure will best fit your particular situation. You can actually incorporate your business without the assistance of an attorney. A corporation is more complicated and expensive to set up. Small corporations can be more informal, but you still must keep accurate records, as corporate officers are liable to their stockholders for what happens in the business.

- **Limited Liability Company (LLC)**: An LLC is not a corporation, but it offers similar benefits. Often, small business owners prefer an LLC to give them the limited liability protection, as well as the tax benefits of a sole proprietor or a partnership. LLCs offer more flexibility in business management and organization.

Products/Services

What products and services do you offer that make you stand out from your competition and create top-of-mind awareness in your client's mind? Look at it from the perspective of the client. What do they want or need?

- In your business plan, explain in detail what products or services you will offer to customers.

- Explain in detail what niche these products and services fill for your customer. It might be that the area is a new, growing area, and families need entire home design services. Perhaps the area you will focus on is custom-designed window coverings; explain why the area needs these services. Give as much detailed information as possible.

- From your research, what products and services are in demand?

- What makes you stand out from the competition? What need are you filling? This will help you form your unique selling proposition (USP), which will be the cornerstone of your marketing plan and message.

Location

If you plan on operating a retail store or studio, then the location you select for your business is critical. You will want to do detailed research on the best location for your business so that it will be convenient for your clients. Choose a location that is easy to find, easy to get in to and out of, and safe. You will want to answer the following questions in your business plan:

- What furniture, fixtures, and inventory is needed at your location?

- How much space will you need?

- Will you have the option to expand if necessary?

- Is the area zoned for your business?

- What are the positive aspects of the neighborhood and the location?

- Is it easily accessible and visible?

- Is it safe? Will you have sufficient lighting for visibility and safety?

- Is the price appropriate for your financial plans?

- Are there complementary businesses near you? Are there businesses near you that are targeting the same customers, but are not direct competition?

Marketing Plan

Your marketing plan is essential to the success of your business. You *must* market your business. To develop a successful marketing plan, start with knowing your clients. In the 1980s, a duo named Al Ries and Jack Trout developed a marketing model that, although expanded upon, still exists today. Ries and Trout said to work from the "bottom up" in developing your plan. Identify your client and what they need; do not just decide that you are going to sell shutters while your customers want custom window coverings. Find out what they want, then find a way you can fill that niche. Develop a marketing plan that will create top-of-mind awareness in the mind of your client of your company whenever they are ready to purchase design services.

Who Are Your Clients?

You can identify your clients by aspects such as age, sex, income, educational level, and location. If you are going to specialize in custom window coverings, you might want to drive around the neighborhoods, looking for homes that have nice cars, nice exteriors, and no or dated window coverings. Do most of the homes have custom or soft window coverings, hard treatments, or shutters? This information will tell you whether these neighborhoods have potential clients who can afford and are in need of your services.

If the thought of creating a marketing plan has you overwhelmed and unable to begin, you might start by answering some thought-provoking questions. Use questions that will make you think about your business as a whole — all the details. If you are purchasing a franchise, the franchisor will have an established plan that you will complete.

Your marketing plan is a subset of your business plan, and you will want to review it constantly throughout the year. You may find you will revise it during the year, or make notes and review it at the end of the year to revise it for the following year.

The following are some questions to get you started:

- Who are your target clients — women, men, or both? Single or married? Professional couples or stay-at-home moms? Perhaps they are in a high-income bracket and work all the time so they have the means to pay for a designer, but do not have the time to do any of the work themselves. The target might be people building new homes, or you might want to focus on people who are renovating their homes. Go into detail identifying your target client.

- Does your target audience fit the area? Meaning, are you targeting new homebuilders in an area that is declining in new home development? Do you wish to reach the wealthy, but are locating your business in a middle-class area?

- What is the condition of the market? Is this the right time to offer your services? Is it the right location?

- Will you be narrowly niched, offering only one type of product, or will you be able to expand your target markets, either by broadening your products and services, or by extending the expanse of your market area?

- Are you priced competitively with your competition? Price does not have to be the defining factor. Often, customer service, quality of work, and quality of the product or service can justify a higher price. In the design business, your creativity and customer service will set you apart from the crowd. You and your competition might sell the same products, so you must differentiate yourself with unique ways of serving your clients.

- What advertising tools are available to assist you in reaching your target audience and creating awareness of what your offer?

- Who is your competition? It is a bit challenging to shop your competition in the world of design, but you can get an idea of what they are doing by reading the paper, looking for press releases on jobs they are working on, and watching their marketing in action. You will also run into clients who have tried your competition, and you can often request feedback from them.

- Who are your closet competitors? Make a list. Also list any indirect competitors. Are your competition's businesses staying steady, growing, or decreasing? Think about the ideas, good and bad, that you get from their advertising or their business. Can you identify their strengths and weaknesses? Use this information to look for a niche you can fill that they are missing.

- What are your competition's products and services? How does this compare to what you are going to offer?

It is a good idea to create a file on each of your competitors. When you come across their ad or any information that talks about an event they sponsored or a job they have, place it in their folder. If you have a client who mentions them, make a note in their file. Review these files from time to time to determine how they are doing. This will also be helpful as you write your marketing plan each year.

Franchise Owners

Does the company require participation in a national marketing fund? Do they assist you with your marketing? Do they help you write your marketing plan? A franchisor will often have a tried and proven marketing method to successfully sell their product and services that you will want to follow. After all, you have purchased a company that is successful; take advantage of their knowledge in how to sell to your clients.

The Product Mix

By now, you are starting to develop your product mix. Your product mix is essentially a list of the services and products you will offer. You will want your business plan to explain what products and services you will offer, how you will achieve this, and why you feel this is the right mix for success in your business and with your target customers.

Advertising and Public Relations

It is not enough to have a good product or service if no one knows about you. You have to create awareness about you, your business, and your product or services. As you develop your marketing plan, you will identify vehicles to carry out the marketing plan. These vehicles are various methods of marketing and public relations. There are many theories on advertising and public relations; take from each what will work for your situation. For example, many people will tell you that word-of-mouth advertising is the absolute best; however, I believe strongly in a marketing mix, meaning you are out there using many different advertising vehicles in an integrated way that creates a consistent image and message. We will discuss specific marketing ideas in detail in Chapter 9.

If you buy a franchise, much of your marketing material will be designed for you with specific suggestions for the best ways to market your business, and you will have paid a premium for this knowledge. Having said that, there are times when your unique location or circumstances may dictate that you deviate from that strict formula. This would be something you could discuss with the marketing department of the franchisor because it is likely that they have other owners who may have similar circumstances. The franchisor wants you to be successful because he or she will make money when you make money. If you have questions or need help with your marketing, ask for your franchisor's help.

In your marketing plan, you will identify the different advertising vehicles and give estimated costs that are associated with these tactics. The sum total of these estimated costs will give you the estimated cost of marketing for your business plan.

Pricing

The goal is to price your product and services so that you can maintain a profit. Are you targeting the wealthy homeowner, the two-income couple with disposable income, or the stay-at-home mom? This information will help you determine your prices. Also consider your net costs for the actual products and the ancillary costs, and factor in your overhead costs. For example, if you sell a sofa to a client, you must factor in your cost of the sofa, the cost of the fabric, any cost related to upholstering, freight, delivery, and sales tax. These are all net costs. Then, you must know what percentage you need to cover your overhead and what net profit you need to stay in business. There are many different ways to price your products in the design industry.

The Management Plan

Do you envision yourself doing everything, or do you know that you will want a design assistant or an in-house bookkeeper? One of the factors that can contribute to the failure of a small business is failure to identify what type of management the company will need. Also, as the owner, you must be honest with yourself in evaluating all the jobs that will be required in your business and determining which ones you are good at and qualified to do, and which ones you are not qualified for, do not want to do, or do not have the time to do.

When you start a small business, you want to save money and do everything yourself. In the beginning, you might be able to do that; however, if you are doing everything, eventually, you will not be able to do everything well. Small business owners tend to be talented at doing what the business does, meaning that as an interior designer, you are creative, talented, and experienced in designing. You may also understand marketing and enjoy doing that, so your marketing will be done well. However, if you are the creative type, you may not be the number cruncher or the best person to handle all the paperwork necessary for a successful design business.

A good owner or manager can give an honest assessment of their abilities, do what they excel at, and hire others to handle the other tasks or outsource them. For example, if you cannot afford both a design assistant and an in-house bookkeeper, you might determine that you need the design assistant to keep you in front of clients on a timely basis and can outsource bookkeeping to your CPA or an independent bookkeeper. I do my own billing and bill paying, but I outsource my quarterly and annual tax returns to my CPA. Your time is valuable, and you should be in front of clients instead of completing tax forms. If you outsource your bookkeeping, make sure you have controls in place so that you know what is going in and out at all times.

If you are doing the billing and payables in-house, consider investing in computerized bookkeeping software, such as QuickBooks®, and learning to read and understand financial statements. They are key tools in knowing where your business is and how it is doing.

Here are some questions to ask yourself that will help you develop your management plan:

- Do you have the background and experience to manage the business end of the business?

- How will you fill in the gaps for the areas where you might be weak?

- Will you hire employees or outsource certain tasks?

- If you decide to hire employees, can you afford the salary and benefit costs?

If you are purchasing a franchise, they may give you direction on management issues. They may have specific requirements; for example, they might have a national accounting or insurance firm that they require you to use. Read all the details of the agreement so that you understand what all your commitments and costs will be.

Financial Management Plan

A realistic budget will be necessary to manage your finances. The financial plan must include start-up costs and operating costs in as much detail as possible. A sound financial plan will contribute to your business remaining profitable. Businesses fail each year because they did not successfully manage their finances. You must develop a realistic financial management plan, learn to read and understand financial statements, and stay on top of the numbers.

Operating Budget

An operating budget will be critical, as you will use it to make decisions about what to pay and when. As you develop your operating budget, you will map out your expenses, the cost of running your business, estimated income, and when expenses need to be paid. The operating budget for purposes of your financial plan within your business plan should include enough money to cover your expenses for three to six months.

The financial plan should include the following information:

- Pending loans
- Inventory
- Up-to-date balance sheet
- A break-even analysis
- A profit and loss statement

When you create your income statement and cash flow projections, create them for the first three years, broken down by month, quarter, and year. These are estimates that may be revised from year to year, but they are a starting place and part of your map to a successful business.

Be realistic on income projections, and err on the side of caution. It is better to understate your anticipated income and be able to cover all your expenses than to commit to expenses based on overinflated income projections. If you are talking to a lender, they will question income projections that seem too optimistic and aggressive. Your CPA, a financial advisor, or the franchisor — if you are purchasing a franchise — may be able to assist you with the financial section of your plan. The Small Business Development Center would also be a valuable asset to you in working on any part of your business plan.

To get an idea of how much start-up money you will need, ask yourself the following:

- How much capital do you have?
- How much will a franchise cost?
- How much will your start-up cost?
- How much money do you need on hand to stay open for business?

If purchasing a franchise:

- Does the franchisor have sales goals you must meet? If so, what are they?

- What sales and profit margins are you expected to reach and maintain? Some will be quite specific, while others will give suggested or recommended goals in this area.

Business Plan Resources

The Small Business Development Center and the information provided in this chapter should keep you from having to develop a plan from scratch and help you create a complete, effective business plan. A well thought-out, well-prepared business plan will not only be a wonderful blueprint to guide you in your business, it will be a valuable tool if you are in need of financing.

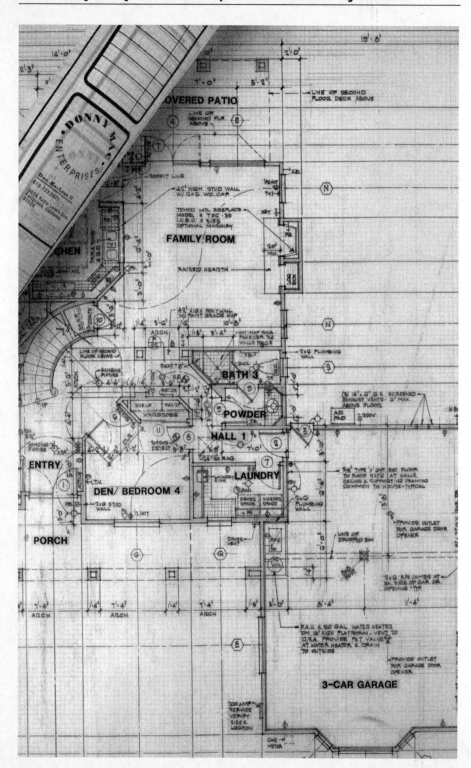

CHAPTER 5

Buying a Franchised Interior Design Business

Definition of a Franchise

Franchised businesses are individually owned businesses that are operated under the name and rules of a large chain, called the franchisor. The franchisor has perfected the successful path of running the business and has created a plan that the franchisees will implement in their business. Everything is standardized with an entire program designed for you from start to finish. If a franchise sells specific products in a retail environment, the owners may be required to sell specific products, in a specific manner, and at a specific price. However, it is a little more complicated with a service-oriented franchise like an interior design or decorating franchise. There are many combinations of products and services that can be sold, and pricing may depend on the area the franchisee is located in. The customer is often buying from the franchisee because of their creativity, customer service abilities, and product mix.

The franchisor is selling the franchisee the right to operate a business using the company's name, logo, reputation, and selling techniques. And in the case of an interior design franchise, the franchisor might sell a franchisee "marketing rights" to certain parts of the country — by zip code, for example. This common practice eliminates competition among owners of the same franchise.

If you purchase a franchise, you will often pay a set sum of money to purchase the franchise and a percentage of gross sales on each sale you make. You may also be required to pay into a national marketing fund. The franchisor may require you to use certain vendors and may require you to purchase marketing materials from them. The franchisor is interested in brand consistency and image in the marketplace, and they may prefer that you use their marketing pieces, or at least follow their marketing standards and guidelines.

Finding a Franchise

There are various ways to find franchise opportunities. You can search on-line for "interior design franchise businesses." Go to **www.franchiseopportunities.com** and **www.franchisegator.com** for information on franchised businesses and to search for design companies. *Entrepreneur* magazine annually gives a list of the top 200 franchised businesses and has many advertisements by franchisors trying to sell franchises. When looking for a design franchise, you may want to try looking in the home design and women-focused magazines for ads for design businesses.

Other ways to research design franchise opportunities include attending a franchise expo, where the franchisors will be set up in trade show format. Just know that there are salespeople at the expo for the purpose of selling the franchise. Prepare yourself to attend the expo with your only goal being to ask questions and obtain information. Purchasing a business is a big decision, and you would not want to make a quick decision. You will want to do your due diligence on any franchised business. To make the most of your expo experience, consider creating a list of questions like the following:

- How long has the company been in business?

- How many franchisees does the company currently have? How many are in your area?

- Is the area you would be interested in available? If not, what areas are available?

- What are the costs, including the initial cost to purchase the franchise, the royalties, and the marketing fees?

- How do the royalty fees work, and how long do you pay them?

- Are the royalty fees a percentage of sales or a set fee?

- What is the marketing fee?

- What assistance will the franchisor give you if you purchase? Is the assistance given just during the start-up phase, or on a consistent basis?

- How much control do you have as a franchisee on what you sell or how you run your business?

- Can you speak to an existing owner? The franchisor will give you names and numbers of owners to contact, but I suggest also finding others on your own and talking to them. Be prepared to ask specific questions of these owners to get a good understanding of what it is like to own the business and work with the franchisor, and what type of sales levels you can expect.

- Ask for any literature that will give you background information on the company.

Investigating the Franchisor

Request a copy of the franchisor's disclosure document, and review it carefully. The Federal Trade Commission has specific requirements regarding companies selling franchised businesses, and they require that this document be given to you ten business days before you sign papers or pay any fees. This is done so that you are not pressured into signing a contract and you have plenty of time to review the document, talk with your attorney, and do any research you need to do to understand the details of the deal.

The disclosure document, called the Uniform Franchise Offering Circular (UFOC), is supplied to pre-qualified franchisees. They are available online, are typically about 50 pages long, and will include many details. Visit the URL **www.nasaa.org/content/Files/UniformFranchiseOfferingCircular. doc** to view the entire document in Word, supplied by NASAA, which is an International Investor Protection Organization. NASAA's form includes the following outline, and any UFOC should include this information:

- Franchisor name

- Business experience of key officials

- Litigation record

- Bankruptcy record

- Initial franchise fee

- Other fees

- Initial investment, including franchise fee, equipment, and any other costs

- Any requirements about where to purchase products and services

- Franchisee's obligations

- Franchisors' obligations

- Territories, including exclusivity and growth options

- Trademarks

- Patents, copyrights, and property information

- Obligation to participate in operating the business

- Restrictions on what franchisee may sell

- Contract renewal, termination and transfers, and dispute resolution

- Earnings claims — estimates of what the franchisee may earn

- List of all franchise outlets, with contact names and numbers

- Franchisor's audited financial statements

- Receipt — signed proof that prospective franchisee received UFOC

- Use of public figures — payment to celebrities or high-profile persons and/or their investment into the system

This document will give you a comprehensive overview of the business, its stability, and the expectations of franchise owners. Study the expectations carefully, as you will be bound by a legal contract to these terms.

Additional Sources of Information

You must do thorough research if considering purchasing any business, especially if you are considering a franchised business. Talk to professionals you trust who will help you further understand the situation of purchasing the franchise.

- **Accountant**: Can help you understand the company's financial statements and earnings projections.

- **Lawyer**: Can review the complicated franchise contract. You will want a clear understanding of the contract that you are signing, as it is almost impossible to make changes after you have signed. It is a legal, binding document.

- **Banker**: Your banker can possibly help you by reviewing the Franchisor's Dunn & Bradstreet reports, which can give you more details on the business.

- **Better Business Bureau**: Check with the BBB® to look for problems or complaints.

- **Federal Trade Commission**: The FTC has business guides that might be helpful in your research.

Advantages of Franchising

There are advantages to owning a franchised business. The franchisor will give you a system that they have developed to use in your business. You are allowed to use the company name, which is already branded and assists you with your business in many ways.

They may assist you in finding a location, provide training, and give you advice on the initial set-up, management, and marketing of your business. There are varying degrees of assistance. Some companies will give you a large amount of assistance up front; others will have continuous assistance available to you. You will want to know this up-front.

It is your job to look at the pros and cons of purchasing a franchise. With a franchise, you can expect that the name has been branded, the general public knows the business, there are already proven systems in place, the marketing might reach farther than you could on your own as an independent design firm, and it may be easier to establish yourself with customers and suppliers. On the other hand, you will be required to give up some control of your business, and you will be in a contractual agreement with the franchisor.

Benefits of Franchising

- **Growth**: They have created name recognition, which may help you grow your business quickly. Being associated with a nationally recognized company may help when you talk to lenders for financing and suppliers for accounts.

- **Experience**: You will be able to draw on the franchisor's experience and knowledge.

- **Consumer recognition**: Brand awareness and name recognition with consumers might give you an edge and instant credibility.

- **Systems and marketing methods**: The company has designed a system that works, and a marketing plan that they supply to you. You are not starting from scratch.

- **Buying power**: You likely gain the benefit of greater buying power due to agreements the franchisor has with suppliers. In the interior design world, it is difficult to get direct accounts with large furniture suppliers, fabric companies, and hard-window-treatment companies. A franchise may open those doors.

- **Training and support**: They have proven techniques, and it is in their best interest to share these with you and train you to manage and promote the business. A good franchisor will be there to help you with all facets of the business.

- **National marketing**: You will reap the benefits of an ad that runs in *Metropolitan* magazine, for example, that you would not be able to afford as an independent design firm. This also sends a message to your customers that you are large and established. However, you must do your own local marketing and promotions.

These benefits are not a guarantee that you will be successful; however, they will likely give you advantages over your competition. If you have never done interior design work before — and a franchise offers training — this would be a wonderful benefit.

Disadvantages of Franchising

You will have to follow the company rules. You are not in complete control of your business. It will not be your name in the logo; it will be the franchised name. There are other issues that you will have to accept with a franchise:

- You will be required to follow their standardized procedures and policies, whether you agree with all of them or not.

- You will share a portion of your gross sales with the franchisor. It is usually a set percentage and is not based on your profit on a sale. This is an additional overhead cost that an independent competitor will not have, and you have to consider this cost of doing business in your margin; in some instances, you must consider whether this will make you less competitive in terms of pricing.

- You may be required to purchase specific items from the company. For example, if the company changes their name or logo, you may be required to purchase new letterhead, envelopes, business cards, and similar items.

- They may require that they approve all of your marketing, ads, promotions, and signs.

- It is possible that the contract will be written to benefit the franchisor. This contract may set high sales quotas, give the company the right to cancel your agreement based on their criteria of what an infringement is, limit your ability to sell your franchise, and otherwise represent their best interests over yours. In this instance, if you have issues or problems with the franchisor, they will have the upper hand in terms of power.

- You can lose your franchise for breaching the contract. They can decide not to renew your contract, and if they do renew your contract, they may have the right to charge a new percentage on the royalty rate. There could be other requirements.

- The contract may allow them to audit your books at any time, and possibly at your expense.

Franchise Financing

The International Franchise Association (**www.franchise.org**) lists more than 30 franchise lenders in their Franchise Opportunities Guide. Also, the U.S. Small Business Administration (**www.sba.gov**) works with banks with guaranteed loan programs for start-up franchisees. Lenders have discovered the potential for growth and stability within the franchise market and are willing to look at financing these ventures.

Evaluating a Franchise Opportunity

There are some unique situations with the design industry — both positive and negative —in terms of franchising. It is difficult to duplicate design

— unlike, say, mufflers. Customers must connect with and trust their designer, whereas customers purchase a muffler based on price. Service affects both types of businesses, but design is quite subjective.

Purchasing a franchise does not guarantee success. You are still ultimately responsible for the daily operation of the business. It is your time and money that is invested, and your ability and talent, that will ultimately determine the success of your business.

CHAPTER 6

Getting Started

Choosing a Name

When you choose the name for your business, you want to catch the attention of your target audience and tell them what you do. Often, the name alone can tell the consumer exactly what you do. For Example, Lisa's Custom Window Treatments tells you exactly what Lisa does — she makes custom window treatments. Lisa might want to simply use her name, but this does not tell anyone what she does. She would want to add a title to the business name that tells people what she does. Lisa's logo could be something like:

- Lisa Doe, Interior Designer — (tells what she does)

- Lisa Doe, A custom window treatment designer — (explains succinctly who Lisa is and what she does)

Names are very important in your marketing plan and the success of your company. Give yourself some time to research what your competition has done with their company names. A name should feel good, sound good, be memorable, and — either alone or with a positioning statement — tell the consumer what the business does.

Home Studio or Retail Space?

To make this decision, you must consider many factors, such as:

- Will you carry inventory, like home accessories?

- Do you want to bring clients to your studio for meetings and presentations?

- Will your budget allow for commercial rent and the additional expenses?

- Are you more comfortable working in a home studio and meeting with clients in their homes?

- Will you be able to get an occupational license to operate your business out of your home?

- Will you be warehousing deliveries of home furnishings yourself, or will you use a receiver?

These are just a few questions to consider when making this big decision. They are designed to get you thinking about whether you need to be in a commercial/retail space or whether working from a home studio will work for you. Obviously, it will save you money to work from a home studio. However, you will need to be highly disciplined and not easily distracted. Hours can slip away quickly, and if you are easily distracted by the TV, dirty dishes, pets, children, neighbors, and other things around you, then you might need to be in an office — although it still might not require a commercial space. You could lease an office, set up your studio there, and still meet with clients in their homes. Some people can work from home quite efficiently, but for others, it is impossible to tune out the distractions. Think about this carefully when making your decision.

Setting Up Your Office

Whether you will be working out of a home office or a commercial office, the following is a list of the basic items you will need to set up your interior design office. First, the basics include:

- **Desk and credenza**: The selection of a desk is a personal preference. You might want an executive desk from the standard office supply store, or you might want a creative, secretarial, open-legged desk that inspires you when you work. Make sure it works for the tasks you will perform at the desk. A credenza gives you additional workspace and space for business files.

- **Task or executive chair**: Look for a comfortable chair, as you will be in it often.

- **File cabinets**: If you have a credenza, you might not need additional filing space when you are just starting out. If you do not have a credenza, you might want a horizontal or lateral file.

- **Drafting table**: This table will adjust on a slant and has a magnifying glass and overhead light. It is helpful for reviewing blueprints and working on layouts and projects.

- **Computer**: The decision is a desktop or laptop, and it is a personal decision. I know some designers who carry a laptop to appointments to show their designs to clients.

- **Printer**: An all-in-one machine might be most economical when first starting out. It would include a fax, copier, scanner, and printer.

- **Telephone**: If in a home office, you will need to decide how many phone lines you will need and whether you will have a true commercial business line for your business, or just a home line. A home line is much less expensive, but you do not get a commercial listing in information or the yellow pages.

- **Fax capability**: You can have a fax machine where you have a dedicated telephone line and number, or you share your telephone line for faxes. There are other options to consider, both for convenience and cost. There are services over the Internet, such as **www.ringcentral.com**, where you can get a local phone number for either your business office phone or fax line, and when someone sends you a fax, you will receive an e-mail from RingCentral® with an attached file, which is a copy of the fax. When you want to fax someone, you scan in the page, or create it in your computer and e-mail it as an attachment to RingCentral and they fax it. These services are much less expensive then hard telephone lines.

- **Internet connection**: Starting out, you might only need a residential DSL connection; however, if you are in a commercial office, you might have to have a business account, which is more expensive than the residential, but also faster.

- **Office supplies**: Including pencils, markers, correction fluid, copy paper, scissors, ruler, pens, stapler, staple remover, sticky notes, and note pads.

Designer Tools

There are software programs that can be purchased or services online that can be used that allow you to create visual design proposals for your clients. Some to look at are:

- **www.DreamDraper.com**
- **www.Icovia.com**
- **www.MinutesMatter.com**

Many designers use a program called AutoCAD for floor plans and layouts.

If you are creating room layouts by hand, you might consider a Magnetic Furniture Kit that allows you to create, in ¼ scale, a room layout with a grid and magnetic furniture pieces that you then photocopy onto your letterhead for presentation. Also, drafting templates — cutout templates of furniture and fixtures — can be used. An architectural ruler will give you different scales, including ¼, ½, and 1 scale.

Another helpful tool is a color wheel. The wheel can help you select complementary colors. You can find them, among other places, at **www.cidinternational.org**.

Samples and Catalogs

All designers' studios are full of samples. Sample books you that you will need include fabric, wallpaper, and trim. You will also need hard window covering samples, including wood blinds and soft shades, as well as catalogs from the vendors you work with. If the vendor has upholstery furniture, you might have a fabric ring of samples available from the supplier. If you use a supplier's fabric, it is usually less expensive than if you send the customer's own material (COM) for the piece of furniture. You will usually pay for these samples unless you reach a set level of spending with the supplier, and you will often be required to buy the samples, and when you hit a certain level of sales with the supplier, they will refund the cost of the samples or rebate it back to you. You may gather many catalogs and samples, and over time, you will begin to see which vendors you are working with and may be able to reduce the amount of catalogs and sample books that you carry.

It is tempting to hold on to all the fabric sample books you can, but if you get quarterly fabric sample books from the supplier, you might want to date the books so that you can get rid of the oldest books, as you will quickly run out of room.

Governmental Requirements

You will need to become familiar with the local, state, and federal laws that will affect you as you start your business. These include registering your business with the state, zoning laws, and applying for occupational licenses.

A good resource for more information is the U.S. Business Advisor's Web site at **www.business.gov**. It includes:

- A business resource library
- The Small Business Administration's start-up advisor
- Online counseling
- Financial resources
- Links to laws affecting different industries
- Legal and regulatory information for small businesses

Here are some other Web sites that you may find helpful:

- The Small Business Administration: **www.sba.gov**

- The IRS: **www.irs.gov/businesses**

- The U.S. Department of Labor: **www.dol.gov/osbp/sbrefa/main. htm**. Go to the eLaws page — **www.dol.gov/elaws** — for employment assistance.

Check your state government Web site for business development information. Some states Web sites will be more user-friendly and organized than others, but most will provide you with forms, state regulations, and much more helpful information. Other resources include your local Economic Development Center, the Chamber of Commerce, or the Small Business Development Center. In some areas, the Small Business Development Center may have business incubators. If you need information on employee guidelines, you might contact the local Equal Employment Opportunity Commission (EEOC) office at 800-669-4000, or log on to **www.eeoc. gov/contact.html** for a listing of their current field offices.

State Registration

Contact the Secretary of State's office in your state as soon as you decide that you want to start a business to find out the details on your state's regulations. Each state has its own regulations. They can give you information about the laws and assist you with contacting your local city and county offices. There is often a state fee to register your business.

Business/Occupational License

The laws vary by state, and even by county and city, but you will likely need to apply for any required occupational licenses for your area. This could include a city and county license, depending on the area and state you are in. You can usually get this information by contacting the local tax collector's office or from the state government. If you want to work from a home studio, be sure you will be in compliance with local ordinances and will be able to get your occupational license.

Zoning

Zoning requirements are designed to monitor the activities going on in certain areas. This helps to keep similar businesses and residences in the same areas. Occasionally, there are exceptions, and you might need to acquire a special permit for a business location. Zoning will impact your parking, sign usage, and the appearance of your building. There might be laws limiting the number of businesses that can be located in a specific area. If you want to locate your business in a historical area, there might be strict restrictions, which will affect you. You will want to check out all of these details *before* you sign a contract. Do not commit yourself in a contract before you are clear on the current zoning requirements and how they will affect your business.

Sales Tax

Most states will require a sales tax ID certificate when you collect sales tax. The taxes could be local, county, and state. Get the details on the state government Web site. Some states may have surcharges for different counties; others may exempt certain things, such as services. This would mean that if you consult with a client, you would not have to charge sales tax, but if you sold them anything tangible, you would be required to collect the tax and forward it to the state. For more guidance, go to your state's Web site for the Department of Revenue. There are many rules, regulations, inspections, and laws that you must be familiar with. The state can do a sales tax audit any time they choose, so you must keep good records.

Federal Identification Number (Employer Identification Number)

All businesses must have a Federal Identification Number. As a sole proprietor, you can use your personal Social Security number, but you are able to acquire a Federal Identification Number, which identifies your business on all tax forms and licenses. To get your number, you must file Form #55-4. To download important publications, go to **www.irs.gov**, or you can call the IRS and request that they be sent to you. The following are some additional forms that will be helpful:

1. Publication # 15, circular E "Employer's Tax Guide."

2. Form W-4, "Employer Withholding Allowance Certificate." Each employee must complete one of these forms. If you pay yourself a payroll check, you must also complete one of these forms.

3. Publication # 334, "Tax Guide for Small Businesses."

Insurance

Most businesses need to address the many aspects of insurance, and an interior design business is no different. There are several types of insurance you should research, including:

- **Property insurance**: This insurance covers equipment, furnishings, and samples you may have stored at your company or home studio. Business property insurance is important when you travel and take merchandise — like carpet samples, window treatments, or even your laptop computer — to your clients' homes.

- **Health insurance**: This insurance can be expensive, and often, small businesses do not offer adequate plans due to the prohibitive costs. Look for a group plan if you are alone or if you employ a small number of people. Associations often offer group insurance plans to their members at some level of discount.

- **Business liability insurance**: This insurance is important for residential and a must for commercial work. If an employee or contractor damages a client's property, the liability insurance will cover it. With commercial projects, the corporation will require a certificate of insurance and will often require certain limits of coverage and to be named as an additional insured. It is easy to meet such requirements: You would contact your agent and give them the requirements of the corporation, and they would forward the certificate directly to the client. Liability insurance will protect you against lawsuits filed by clients who may not be happy with your services. There is a category called employment practice liability insurance. Many lawsuits are filed against big companies, but even small design firms can get sued. This insurance covers sexual harassment, discrimination, wrongful termination, breach of employment contract, failure to employ or promote, wrongful discipline, deprivation of career opportunity, wrongful infliction of emotional distress, and other areas. If you employ more than a few people, you might want to consider this insurance.

- **Auto insurance**: If you have a logo-ed vehicle and/or use a vehicle for business, which might include delivering products and samples to clients' locations, you might want to consider commercial auto insurance. This is the most expensive auto insurance — if you use your personal auto, and it is not logo-ed, you might be better with just a personal auto policy. Either way, if you are working on a commercial project, your client will require a copy of the declarations page, certain levels of coverage, and to be named as an additional insured.

- **Workers' compensation insurance**: This insurance has been an item of controversy for many years. It can be so expensive that a small business cannot afford it, but it is required. In some states, like Florida, for instance, if you are the only employee and the owner, you can get a certificate of exemption from the state. Commercial clients will require a copy of the exemption or the policy for any project. Also, if you have employees, this insurance will cover you if an employee gets injured on the job, whether in your place of business or on a job site.

- **Business interruption insurance**: What would you do if a flood or fire destroyed your business? Business interruption insurance will cover this and is usually added to property insurance, not sold separately.

Do some research and compare policies and prices. It might be easier to contact brokers who represent several insurance companies and have them do the comparisons for you. There is a franchised insurance firm called Brightway Insurance^{SM} that they can often save you money on your policies. It is efficient for you to have all your plans through one broker because when you have an insurance issue, there is one contact person.

You can also contact the Independent Insurance Agents and Brokers of America®, at 1-800-221-7971, or go to **www.iiaba.net**, where you can find information about different types of insurance, new trends, and laws.

Payroll Taxes

There are other taxes to be aware of, besides sales tax, including the following:

- **Income tax**: This can include federal, state, and local taxes. If you have employees, or if you pay yourself a payroll check, you are required to withhold federal income tax. These taxes are deposited with the government on a set schedule. When you hire an employee, they must complete a W-4 form, which is the Employee

Withholding Allowance Certificate where the employee chooses which level of level of taxes they wish to be withheld from their paycheck. At the end of the year, you must complete a W-2 to show income paid to your employees and the taxes that were withheld. This form must be mailed by January 31. If you use computerized accounting software, the software will gather this data, and you will merely need to print the forms, or if you have a CPA do your end-of-year taxes, they can print and mail them out for you. A copy goes to the employee, you keep a copy for your records, and a copy of all the W-2s is submitted with your return, under a W-3 form, to the IRS.

- **FICA taxes**: These taxes are also withheld by the employer from the employee and paid to the federal government. These taxes cover Social Security and Medicare for you and any employees you have. The company withholds half from the employee and must pay the other half. You match the amount withheld from the employee and send the total in to the federal government.

To send these taxes, you will receive a coupon booklet from the government, and you are required to use the coupons form 501. You pay these taxes through any commercial banking institution that is authorized to accept these tax deposits from your business.

Contractors are treated differently. There are specific guidelines that you must use to determine whether someone is contract labor or an employee. The IRS watches this, as it can be abused by businesses not wanting to pay their portion of taxes or benefits. If you hire a contract installer to install window treatments, you must have that person complete form W-9 each year. If they are not a corporation, you will need to file form 1099 each year to report the amount of money paid to that person that year. If you have paid a contractor less than $600, you are not required to file a 1099, but if you paid them more than $600, you must file the form and report all the payments. A copy goes to the person, a copy stays in your records, and a copy is sent to the federal government. The contractor is responsible for paying all the associated taxes. Be familiar with the rules on this and follow them. If the government decides that a contractor is actually an employee, you, as the employer, will pay taxes and fines for this error.

Taxes can be confusing and overwhelming for business owners, so I recommend that you spend some time reviewing the Web site **www.irs.gov**. You will find a tax calendar on the accompanying CD-ROM for your use. The calendar features these three federal taxes:

1. Income tax withheld from employees' wages or non-payroll amounts paid

2. Social Security and Medicare taxes (FICA taxes) from employees' wages and the Social Security and Medicare taxes that you pay as an employer

3. Federal unemployment (FUTA) tax that your business must pay

The calendar lists dates to file returns and when to make deposits for these taxes. Review IRS Publication 15, which outlines deposit rules. You may need the following forms:

*   **Form 940 (or 940 EZ)**: Employer's Annual Federal Unemployment (FUTR) Tax Return. This is due annually, one month after the calendar year ends. It is used to report your FUTR tax.

*   **Form 941**: Employer's Quarterly Federal Tax Return. You will file this form one month after the end of each quarter. This form is used to report Social Security and Medicare taxes and federal income taxes withheld on employee wages.

CHAPTER 7

Internal Bookkeeping

At this point, you probably have your permits and occupational licenses, and all the required state and federal paperwork has been completed. You have found the proper insurance and are ready to get started. It is time to set up an efficient way to keep track of the money that comes in and the expenses that are paid. It is critical to know your expenses, when they are due, and when you will receive money.

Budgeting

Internal bookkeeping will include any financial transactions. As you receive bank statements, you will want to review them and balance them so that you know that they are accurate. Even if you choose to hire an accountant to do some of this work, it is critical that you stay personally involved with the internal financial and daily details, as this will allow you to identify potential problems early.

You might consider hiring a part-time bookkeeper. This person will be trusted with handling your accounting books and your money, so you want to feel confident in their trustworthiness. A bookkeeper will generally enter your sales, create client invoices (account receivables), enter vendor bills (accounts payable), and pay vendors. The accounting software discussed earlier will allow you to print and review a variety of reports that will help you track income and expenses and see what is being done.

Once a week, you might want to review the accounts payable report to know who you owe and how much money you need to pay them, and an aged accounts receivable report to understand what clients owe you money and how old that invoice is. Another valuable report is a cash flow report. Finally, as discussed previously, you should have a good understanding of how to read and interpret financial reports, such as a balance statement and a profit and loss statement. They are good overviews of where the business is financially, and if you have budget numbers plugged into your software program, you can see if you are on track with your budget.

Accounting Software

Go to **www.quickbooks.com** for more information on the QuickBooks software. This program has payroll and inventory features that can be quite helpful. I use QuickBooks in my businesses and find it easy to use and detailed. You can customize reports for your purposes.

Another popular accounting program is Peachtree® (**www.peachtree.com**). It also offers a variety of features. You might want to review several programs and determine which offers the best features for your needs and comfort level. You might want to consider which programs your accountant, if you are working with one, prefers to use. My CPA uses QuickBooks, so I make a backup each quarter and take it to him. It makes it easy and efficient for him, which saves me money.

Managing Your Cash Flow

You need to know in an instant how much money you have on hand and whether there is enough money to pay bills, suppliers, payroll, and other expenses. Paying bills on time can save you money. Some suppliers offer a percentage discount if you pay by a certain day of the month. Staying on top of the bills will save you money by avoiding penalties and interest.

As a start-up business, you will likely be required to pay in advance or with a credit card for a period of time in order to establish credit terms. Once you are established, your suppliers might give you 30 day terms, or 30 days to pay. Some, however, will always require either full payment up-front, or 50 percent up-front and the balance before they ship the order. In turn, I request a 50 percent deposit from my clients when the contract is signed and the balance upon installation. Often, the full 50 percent goes toward the cost of goods, and some of the balance pays the final amounts due. I often do not see any of the profit until the job is completed and I receive final payment.

Freight companies are different in that some will require cash on delivery (COD), while others will allow you to set up terms. It will be to your advantage to establish terms with a few freight companies, as they will often be delivering to your receiver — a company that receives, stores, and delivers your items for you so that you do not have to pay for your own warehouse space — and the receiver will not pay a COD for you.

Getting Paid

In the design business, you are often dealing with large amounts of money for the projects you do, and you cannot produce custom products over-night, so asking for full payment up front is not logical. However, as I mentioned above, a 50 percent deposit is normal, and I recommend it. Consider that when you are working on a commercial project, you are working for a large corporation, and often, the project will be a substantial one. Your small business cannot serve as a bank for the large company by paying for all the items up front and waiting for payment. It is reasonable to request a deposit due to the nature of how suppliers might work with you, requiring deposits or full payments up front, and requiring the balance the day of installation.

Payment Methods

You may offer your customers a few payment options. They may pay by check or credit card, or you can offer them terms — I only recommend this for commercial or corporate clients, and then based on 50 percent down and balance due upon installation. If you decide to accept credit card payments, you, as the vendor, will pay a percentage of the sale to the credit card company, and there are fees associated with the company that processes the transactions. You will want to shop around for the best deal on processing these payments.

When accepting checks, have your procedures in place. Each state has "bad check" laws, and you might want to use these rules in your business. There are also confirmation systems for checks. They confirm that the money is available, and some even hold the funds for you until the check clears the bank. You will pay for this service, but it can save you money in the long run. For example, often, once you place a custom order with a furniture supplier, it is non-refundable or cancellable — meaning that if your client has given you a bad check, you will still be responsible for paying for the orders placed with your suppliers. For more information, you can go to **www.checkfraud.com.**

CHAPTER 8

Budgeting & Operational Management

Most successful businesspeople develop detailed budgets and work to adhere to them. It is easy to create a budget, but more difficult to stick to it. However, you have a greater chance of success if you stick to your budget. A business also needs a long-range financial plan. You can create a financial plan annually, as these tools will allow you to estimate the amount of income your business should generate and the amount of expenses that you will be obligated to pay. Break it down into monthly budgets to make it easier to manage and to allow you to budget for fluctuations in revenues and expenses.

For example, factories basically close for two weeks at Thanksgiving and Christmas. Knowing this, there will be a cut-off date at which point you will have to tell your client that they will not receive their items before the holidays. Business in design slows down around Thanksgiving because of this and because people are paying attention to the holidays. Also, factories might be on limited capacity during the large furniture markets, as most of their staff will be at market; this will put their production schedules behind, which can cause a slow down for you in terms of income.

Professional Fees

Legal: You will need legal advice at times. Consider budgeting a little each month for these fees so that if you need to use your attorney, you will have budgeted for this expense.

Accounting: If you are using a CPA, either monthly or quarterly, you will want to budget accordingly for these fees. They should be set amounts with no surprises, unless you have additional work at times throughout the year.

Utilities

The following are the typical types of utilities you will want to include in your budget:

Telephone: The charges should be pretty consistent each month. This category should also include your cell phone bill.

Water and Electric: If you have set up a retail location, you will either have water and electric included in your rent, or you will pay them yourself, as you will if you purchase the building you are in. If you work from your home, you may want to consult with your accountant about the pros and cons of taking home office deductions. If you choose to take them, you are allowed to deduct a percentage of these bills. There are some ramifications if you take the home office deductions regarding the value or resale value of your home, so you want to be sure it is a good decision for your situation. Also, be prepared for scrutiny from the IRS if your deductions seem abnormal. It could raise a red flag to target you for an audit.

Fixed Operating Costs

Rent or mortgage payment: These will not apply if you are working from home. Otherwise, you will want to budget for these expenses monthly.

Insurance: I take my annual cost of my insurance policies and divide them by twelve so that I can budget a portion each month for this expense.

Taxes: This includes property taxes, if applicable, and again, you want to estimate all your taxes and budget a monthly amount.

General Operating Costs

These are a few examples of general operating costs to consider:

Entertainment: The IRS rules are quite specific about what is deductible. If you are entertaining a client and discussing business, you can deduct the expense. Be sure to keep the receipt and write the name of the client, business discussed, and date on it, and keep the record in case you are audited.

Travel: Business travel with receipts and notes, as described above for entertainment, is advisable.

Advertising: This includes all expenses associated with marketing and advertising, such as Web site, TV ads, print ads, radio spots, direct mail, fliers, imprinted promotional items, and event sponsorships.

Postage: Stamps and/or postage meter.

Contributions: Include all contributions the business makes to a recognized charitable organization.

Dues and Subscriptions: Dues to professional organizations, such as ASID, The Builders Association, the Chamber of Commerce, and all others should be included here. Trade magazine subscriptions can also be included here.

Licenses: This would be all of your business and government licenses. This includes your occupational license and state licensing fee, if one is required in your state for you to practice interior design.

Credit card fees: If you accept credit cards, you want to record the monthly service charges and the percentage you are charged for your credit card charges, as well the rental fee for the machine.

Auto: If the business owns the vehicle, include the monthly payment, or if you use your personal auto and reimburse yourself or employees for mileage, include that here.

Interest: If you pay interest on a mortgage payment, record it here.

Bad Debt: You hope you will not have to use this account, but realistically, you never know, so set it up. You can deduct it on your taxes.

Depreciation: If you have a retail store, you might have more equipment and fixtures that can be depreciated. If you have a home studio, you might have less. The IRS allows you to "depreciate" the cost of an asset over a certain amount of time, which gives you a tax break. The IRS has guidelines for the number of years to be used for calculating an asset's useful life. Your accountant can advise you on the rules, and the depreciation can be calculated at the end of the year in time for tax preparation by your accountant.

Cost of goods: This account is used to record the net cost of any items you purchase for a project.

Shipping and freight: Record all freight costs and shipping costs in this expense category.

There will be other expenses that you will come across, and as you do, add these to your budget.

Employees

Many designers start out on their own with no employees. You may quickly find that as business grows, you need to hire an assistant, other designers, or office staff. When you purchase a business, you might be starting out with employees. As your business grows, your time will quickly be all used up. In order to continue growing, you can either raise your rates or add employees, which will allow your company to take on more work and grow.

Be certain that you correctly identify anyone working for you — meaning, they are either an employee or a subcontractor. An employee receives a paycheck with taxes withheld by the company and has set work hours and job duties. A subcontractor would be your installers, for example; they are not employees. They work for themselves, and you contract out the work to them. They give you an estimate or price for the work, and you pay them the fee. They are then responsible for paying their own taxes. You will be required to send W-2s to your employees at the end of the year, as well as file them with the IRS. You will send a 1099 form to any subcontractors whom you pay $600 or more in a calendar year. You are also required to file these with the IRS.

When an employee is hired, he or she should complete a W-4 Employees Withholding Allowance Certificate form. When you work with any vendor, you must require them to complete a W-9. It will tell you whether they are incorporated, in which case you are not required to send them a 1099 at the end of the year. If they are not incorporated, then you must send the 1099 if they are paid $600 or more in the calendar year. You can find these forms at **www.irs.gov**. The IRS is quite specific on what constitutes an employee or a subcontractor. You can use form SS-8-Determination of Worker Status for Purposes of Federal Employment Taxes and Income Tax Withholding. It can be found at **www.irs.gov/pub/irs-pdf/fss8/pdf.** If the IRS determines that someone should have been treated as an employee, you will have to pay back payroll taxes, interest, and penalties. It is essential that you know the rules on how to determine whether someone is an employee or a subcontractor.

Selecting Vendors and Manufacturers

You want to work with reliable manufacturers and vendors, and you want to sell quality products. You will constantly be looking at new vendors and suppliers, but in the beginning, it will take some time on your end to find the ones you will start with. You can contact the company directly, and they will put you in contact with the manufacturer representative. Meet with them and let them explain their products and how you can become a client. Ask plenty of questions about product, quality, pricing, promotions, cost of sample materials and catalogs, and anything else you can think of. Often, a good relationship with a rep can make the difference between a decent experience with the company and an incredible experience. If you have problems with a product, the rep can be your best bet on getting the problem resolved.

When you attend furniture and accessory markets, you can use that time to meet with your existing vendors and search for new ones as well. This gives you the opportunity to see and touch their products, check out the latest products, and often pick up a catalog. The markets can be good places to get new ideas, products, and suppliers.

The Internet has been embraced by the design industry and often, a supplier will have an in-depth Web site. You will have to be a customer and be given a login, but you can often look for products, look up pricing, and use the photos of products for your client presentations — all on the vendor Web site.

You will find that whether you are small and just starting out, or a larger firm, working with a handful of quality suppliers that have the products you need will be of great benefit to you. Doing this will give you stronger buying power by concentrating your spending with a few suppliers, versus buying a little from everywhere. You will also save money on catalogs and samples if you are only purchasing from a few suppliers. Many will rebate the cost of these items back to you after you reach a certain sales quota in a year. Samples are essential to the sales process.

You will want to select a few fabric lines and meet with the rep of each line. Ask for sample books, but be prepared that you might have to purchase the books. This is true in the wallpaper industry, where they rarely give away any sample books. They have "book programs" where you are shipped the books once a quarter and charged for them. They do this because the cost of sample books is quite high.

There will be times when it makes sense for the client's budget to buy retail. It never hurts to ask the store whether they give a designer discount. Some will not offer any; others will give a discount; and still others will pay a "back-end" commission to you. There will also be times when you just cannot use your regular vendors. They might not have the product you need, or the price point might be too high. That is when it is nice to have created a relationship at market with other vendors.

If you are going to sell furniture, it can be difficult as a small design firm without retail space to even get an account with the large furniture companies. They will often require a certain amount of their product to be purchased and displayed in a retail showroom, or they will require a certain spending level annually in order to have an account with them. There are ways to work around this, but it can be challenging. You can find smaller companies at market that have furniture and accent furniture pieces. For upholstery pieces, you can find companies that make "generic" pieces, and you send them your own fabric (COM) — client's own fabric. The only time you might have to purchase from a retail furniture store is if you have a client that definitely wants a specific name-brand furniture line and you cannot establish an account directly with them. You can talk with the furniture store about any designer discounts they offer. Some will also sell at retail and send you a rebate or commission check on the sale.

Accessory accounts are fairly easy to set up. There are usually small minimum order requirements, and you might have to pay up front for the first few orders, but you may then be eligible to establish an account with terms. "Terms" means that you place an order, they ship the order and bill you, and you have 30 days to pay the bill. This is commonly referred to as "net 30" terms. If you use a credit card for your purchases, you might consider using one that accumulates mileage rewards. They might pay for your ticket to market. Of course, with credit cards, I recommend you use them to get those reward miles and pay them off every month so that you are not paying interest on the balance.

Document your dealings with your vendors. I suggest you place orders with a purchase order. If you are working manually, you can purchase generic purchase orders at the office supply stores. If you are using a program like QuickBooks, it will have a purchase order form you can complete and fax or e-mail to the vendor. You will want to give specific directions on where to deliver, the date you need the products, and the actual item numbers and quantity of the product you are ordering. The vendor should send you a confirmation. You might make a note on your calendar to follow up on that paperwork — if you do not get a confirmation, the order could have been lost. When it is close to delivery time, you might follow up with the vendor to confirm delivery is still on track.

Also, when working on proposals, it is a good idea to check with the vendor to confirm that the products you are going to present to your client are still available and are not discontinued, have not had a price change, and are not on back-order. Do this even with fabric because once you show clients a fabric or piece of furniture they love, it will be hard to make them happy with a substitute.

CHAPTER 9

Marketing Your Business

"Marketing is the activity, set of institutions, and processes for creating, communicating, delivering, and exchanging offerings that have value for customers, clients, partners, and society at large."

— *American Marketing Association*®

As a small business owner, you might find that the word "marketing" is sometimes overwhelming, and some owners might not understand just how important marketing is to their business. But marketing is essential; you have to let people know that you are out there. You are fighting for a place in the mind of the consumer, and you secure that place with marketing.

You do not have to have a huge budget to effectively market your business, but it will take planning, money, creativity, and time. An integrated marketing mix will allow you to brand your business and yourself; create top-of-mind awareness with the consumer; and reach your target audience.

Choosing a Name

We touched on this briefly earlier, but a name is critical for success. The name should reflect who you are and what you do. If the company name cannot clearly communicate what you do, add a positioning statement.

Often, designers will use their name with the word "design," "firm," or "associates" after it to create a business name. If you intend on branding yourself, think about down the road if you decide to sell your business and how this will positively or negatively affect your ability to sell the business.

Hiring an Expert

You may feel overwhelmed with creating a marketing plan. If you feel you need assistance, you might consider hiring an advertising or public relations firm. I would suggest that you find a small firm that will give you personalized attention. If you do not have a large marketing budget, you might get lost in a large advertising firm. Agencies will work for an hourly rate or on a project basis, and if they place advertising for you, it is customary that you will pay a 15-percent agency fee on the cost of the advertising placed on your behalf. Often, the media outlets will charge you the same amount whether you or your agency pays for it, but if the agency places the ad, the media will "discount" the charge by 15 percent to the agency, which is how the agency gets their 15 percent.

The following are some of the services that they can offer:

- **Develop your image**: This approach uses logo, positioning statement, and brand.

- **Create your advertising message**: This should be an integrated, consistent message that best conveys what you do and who you are and is designed to reach your target audience.

- **Develop advertising campaigns**: The agency will suggest the media and advertising vehicles that will best serve you in your marketing mix to reach your audience.

- **Design and produce**: The agency will create print, TV, radio, and web pages or web ads.

- **Place media buys**: The agency can purchase ad time or space for your business and manage it for you so that it frees you up to design.

If your budget will not allow you to hire a full-service agency, there are other options, such as hiring a freelance marketing consultant, freelance graphic artist, and freelance copywriters. If you go this route, you will have to invest more time and leadership to manage the projects.

When looking for freelance experts, look for people with the following:

- Knowledge of and experience with design firms
- Willingness to work with your budget
- Client referrals

Working with a good advertising agency can save you time and, in the long run, money because if you are not comfortable managing the marketing plan, you may make costly mistakes. An agency can create a consistent brand, image, and an integrated marketing strategy for your business.

Doing it Yourself

Before you decide to go it alone, do your research. You can get assistance from the Small Business Development Center on understanding marketing and advice along the way as you create and implement your marketing plan. I will give you suggestions throughout this chapter on ways to successfully market your design business, even if you do not have any marketing experience. These are just a few resources that can help you get started:

- Constant Contact® (**www.constantcontact.com**), an e-mail marketing service that can keep you in touch with your customers and potential customers. They provide user-friendly services for creating an e-zine or electronic newsletter. Another cost-effective e-mail service is Got Marketing® (**www.gotmarketing.com**).

- You can learn about marketing techniques at Market It Right^{SM}, at **www.marketitright.com**.

- Look at Idea Site for Businesses at **www.ideasiteforbusiness.com** for creative marketing ideas.

Guerilla Marketing

Jay Conrad Levinson is the creator of Guerilla Marketing, which is a method of marketing that empowers small business owners to effectively market their businesses without spending a fortune. Levinson has marketing and PR books, business tools, and a Web site (**www.gmarketing.com**) that give you step-by-step, hands-on, practical advice on marketing your business on a minimum budget.

The following are a few of the books and CDs you may find useful as you design your own "Guerilla Marketing" plan:

Books

- *Guerrilla Publicity*

- *Guerilla Advertising*

- *Guerilla Marketing Excellence*

- *Guerilla Marketing 101*

- *Guerilla Marketing in 30 Days*

- *Guerilla Marketing: Secrets for Making Big Profits from Your Small Business*

- *Guerrilla Publicity: Hundreds of Sure-Fire Tactics to Get Maximum Sales for Minimum Dollars*

- *Guerrilla Marketing Excellence: The 50 Golden Rules for Small Business Success*

Compact Disc

- *Guerilla Marketing for Franchises*

Most of Levinson's "guerilla marketing" ideas are low-cost marketing methods for your business to use. Go to his Web site, **www.gmarketing.com**, for more information.

Advertising Vehicles

Traditional advertising is a purchased space or time where your ad runs in various media. Be careful and selective, or you will find yourself spending tons of money and not seeing a return on your investment. First, you will need to identify who your target audience is; then, determine which advertising vehicles will effectively reach this audience, and finally, which ones will do this for the best price. You will be bombarded with advertising sales representatives contacting you and wanting to meet with you. They will all tell you how great they are, how they will reach your target audience, and how they can give you the best bang for your buck. They will try to create a sense of urgency for you to sign the contract and advertise with them.

Do your own research. First determine your target audience, then research the various methods of advertising to determine which will be the most effective for your business. Another suggestion I would make is to try and plan your advertising for the year so that you will not be constantly reacting to every rep who calls with the next greatest advertising opportunity. You will be able to say that your advertising plan is in place for the year and, instead of meeting with them, that they can send you information for consideration for next year.

Here are a few suggestions on how to gather information about your "ideal customer" or your target audience:

- Know your competition. How do they market, where do they advertise, and what type of service do they give their customers?

- Familiarize yourself with trade publications. These magazines can be a wealth of information. One great publication is *Vision Magazine*, and American Society of Interior Designers® (ASID), an industry association, has a great newsletter.

- Use your franchisor as a resource. If you purchased a franchise, the franchisor will have detailed information on your ideal customer.

An Effective Logo

Logos can be crucial. You will want a professional graphic artist to create it for you. Be aware that some graphic artists are excellent at creating the logo but do not know how to direct the project meaning; they do not have the marketing principles they need to develop the concept needed for your logo. Logos can be simple or highly creative. If your company name is mostly your name, it can be treated graphically with custom fonts. Also, icons in a logo are common and can also help relay your company image. Your logo should be on everything you do.

I have a unique suggestion for a way to get or create logo for little investment. I have done this in the past, and it was a big success. Go to your closest university or college and talk to the head of the department that offers graphic design courses. You want to set up a contest for the graphic design students to create a logo for your business. You will give them all the information on who you are, what your business does, and who your target audience is. You might want to make sure you tell them how the logo will be used, as you want one that can easily be printed on your brochure and promotional products. Remember that a one- or two-color logo will be less expensive to print than a full four-color design.

Then, you have a deadline for entries. They present their logos and explain what they did and why they did it that way. You pick first-, second-, and third-place winners. Then, you give the first-place winner $250, the second-place winner $150, and third-place winner $75. You make those awards in front of the class. You can then write a press release with a photo of the class and the new logo and send it to your local media. It is a good local story about education, and it is likely that not only will they at least print it, but they may also write a story about it. The other positive aspect is that all the students have another piece for their portfolio to show to potential employers. It is a win/win for everyone — especially for you.

Business Cards and Brochures

Once you have a business name and logo, your next step is business cards and possibly a company brochure or flier. You can print information on the front and back of your business cards. Hand them out freely, as they can be one of the most cost-effective advertising methods. Business cards are an inexpensive way to market your business. You can get 5,000 business cards printed for under $200 on many online gang-run print companies, such as **www.vistaprint.com**, where you can even get free business cards. The catch is that you are limited to generic templates. For a cost of something like three cents a card, you can upgrade the design and/or paper for a more customized card. Additionally, there are many printing Web sites that offer inexpensive printing of business cards and brochures. You do not need an agency to handle your printing because they will add a margin onto the printing price. When the printer designs your print pieces, make sure that you own the works so you can have them send the graphic files to any printer you choose. Make the most of your business cards. Have your logo, name, contact phone numbers, e-mail address, and Web address. Print your Web address on everything, including your ads: Having a Web address in today's business world is a necessity.

Brochures or fliers can be a good leave-behind piece and a good marketing piece to place in other businesses that your target audience frequents — with their permission, of course. They can be mailed to a prospect after you have made the appointment but before they meet with you. Again, these can be printed quite inexpensively, so shop around for printing prices. If you do not know any freelance graphic artists, check out **www.sologig. com**. There are other sites that allow you to post your project on their sites, and graphic artists can bid on the project. Check out **www.elance.com** and **www.guru.com**.

Neighborhood Marketing

This is a concept that has been around for a while, and it is highly effective. You go to businesses such as restaurants, gas stations, and pizza shops that are in the area where your target audience frequents and ask whether you can place your business cards and/or brochures in their business. I often place mine in doctors' offices, plastic surgeons' offices, and spas because they are looking for the same audience that I am looking for. You might offer to go in with one of these businesses and hold a design workshop or do a joint promotion or mailing. Neighborhood marketing is about working with other complementary businesses in your community and getting your name out to their customers.

Gift Certificates

I use gift certificates as giveaways at networking events, at silent auctions, and to thank existing customers. You can have a custom gift certificate printed, or use a generic one that can be found at the office supply stores. People can purchase a gift certificate as a gift for someone else.

Web Site

Many small businesses feel that they do not need a Web site and that it is too cost-prohibitive. But in today's business world, you might not be considered a professional business if you do not have a Web site. As an interior design firm, it will mostly be an awareness page, creating the image of your company, telling the consumer what you offer and what your design philosophy is, and showing some of your portfolio work. I would also strongly recommend adding testimonials, as well as before-and-after photos of the work you have done. Keep your Web site updated by adding press releases about new projects, charitable events you participate in, and any other news about your company. You could also consider creating a design blog on your site. Give information on design. People cannot get enough how-to information on design. Make it easy for prospects to contact you. Make sure your phone number, e-mail address, and street address — if you are a retail business — are easy to find on the page.

If you keep fresh information on your Web site, people will come back to it. Also, you can use the site as a way to capture leads. For example, you might give away a free design trends report. They must register to get this, and you should ask whether they wish to receive your newsletter. You then have their information and can send your e-zine or printed newsletter to them.

E-zines are quite popular. It can be overwhelming to think of creating this on your own, so you might consider a company that allows you a way to easily create and send your e-zine. One such company is **www.constant-contact.com**. When creating an e-zine, keep it short and simple, and you only send it out quarterly, or perhaps monthly; you do not have to send it weekly. If you are in touch too much, people may block you. Remember that you do not want to send nothing but an advertisement. You want to give tips, ideas, and information that people will want to read. Shop around for a company to create your Web site that understands your business and your needs for a Web site; compare prices. The type of Web site discussed is simple and should not be too expensive to create.

Regarding the domain name of your site, try to find your business name. Be careful that you do not have too long of name, or a difficult name to remember or spell. During the early dot-com era, businesses tried to be clever with web address names and would use a name that had nothing to do with the name of their business. People found them hard to remember because they did not have anything to associate them with. This is an important decision; give it some thought and get some advice from either your advertising agency or the company creating the site for you. Give the designer some guidance on what you want on your site. You can research your competition and other design firms, large and small, around the country and the world, to see what they do on their sites.

Make sure that your web address is printed on everything you do. Your business card, your brochure, your ads — print it on everything. It establishes credibility and is an integrated approach to your marketing efforts.

Networking

Some people have no stress over networking, while others find it quite uncomfortable. If it does not stress you out, you might consider joining a networking group. There are national networking groups, such as Business Networking International (BNI®), which is the largest networking organization in the world, that have local chapters, and there are local networking groups. Be sure you understand the rules before joining. For example, groups like BNI will not allow more than one person per industry in each group, and you cannot miss more than two meetings or you are out. These are serious networking groups.

There are other, more subtle, networking groups. You could join the local Chamber of Commerce and attend events such as Business after Hours. You might want to join a young professionals group or even a charitable organization; you will likely find these are good ways to network. You can even network at church, at social events, and with any organized group or association. It is a good idea to always keep in mind a ten-second and a 30-second "commercial" about your business for networking purposes. This makes you think hard about what would best tell people what you can do for them. Such quick self-advertisements are effective networking tools. Some groups to consider that are not intensive business networking groups would be the women's club, the garden club, and other groups where you might meet your target audience.

Seminars

Design seminars are a good way to reach out to potential customers and to position yourself as an expert in the field of design. You can create Microsoft® PowerPoint® presentations of:

- Best window treatments
- Before-and-after room designs
- How-to presentations, such as how to paint, wallpaper, or choose appliances

Your seminar can be as simple or as elaborate as you want it to be. You could have a fun night, bring in someone who will do "mini manicures," serve nice appetizers, and even tie the event in with a charity.

My suggestions for a successful event are:

- Make it fun

- Share information for free

- Do not try to sell anything at the event

- Have door prizes

- Have visuals and samples — people love to touch and feel fabrics

- Have your appointment book and your portfolio

- Have goody bags that include a small token gift, a business card, and a brochure to send home with your guests

- Ask for their contact information in order to register for door prizes

Example Photos *from*
Interior Designers

The following photos are contributed by Interiors Northwest.

Before

After

❧ The following photos are contributed by Bonnie Sachs. ❧

Before

After

Before

After

✢ The following photos are contributed by RC Design. ✢

Before

After

After

Before

After

❖ The following photos are contributed by Jane Speroff. ❖

Before

After

Before   *After*

Before

After

The following photos are contributed by Stacy Lapuk. ❖

Before   After

Before   After

Before

After

❧ *The following photos are contributed by Appliegate Tran Interiors.* ❧

Before

After

After

Before

After

Before

After

- Practice what you will say and your presentation so that you are relaxed and knowledgeable when you are in front of your guests

- For your location, you can partner with a complementary business that has the space or use a clubhouse

You can advertise in your newspaper ads, use direct mail, and send out press releases to announce the event. Create urgency by requiring a call to RSVP because space is limited.

Direct Mail

Direct mail is a good piece for your marketing mix. The postcard-printing companies you can find online offer the lowest prices for large orders of 4x6 postcards. The site **www.opportunityknocks.com** can have each postcard addressed personally to the home owner and target a specific area. Direct mail includes the cost of designing the piece, printing, and a service that handles the mailing for you. They can sell you a mailing list, based on the criteria you give them — area, household income, and other issues — or use your mailing list, create labels, and prepare them for the post office. It is less expensive to use a bulk-mail permit number than to mail them first-class. The normal success rate of direct mail is a 1- to 2-percent response, which is why direct mail is usually used to mail to a large amount of people.

Another good way to use direct mail is for new home buyers. I subscribe to a company that, by zip code, sends me mailing labels for the people who have purchased homes. I receive the labels weekly, and I mail them a postcard. If they have just purchased a home, they may need some or all of my services. If they are new to the area, I want them to know that I exist and can help them with their design needs. The following are some resources to look at for your direct mail needs:

- The Direct Marketing Association: **www.the-dma.org**

- Home Owners Marketing Services: **www.homeown.org**

- Melissa Data®: A mailing list and direct mail service, **www.melissadata.com**

Existing Customers

It costs less to keep your existing customers than it does to find new ones, so do not forget your existing customers in your marketing mix, but include them in your mailing list so that they receive all your marketing pieces and newsletter, if you send one out. Call them and touch base. Ask whether they need anything or whether they have projects they are considering in the future, and ask them for referrals.

If you have a seminar, invite them. Consider doing a customer appreciation event. It could be a small reception where you can mingle and just say "thank you" for their business. Think of a small holiday gift in December, and even keep track of their birthdays, sending cards. Find ways to stay in touch with them throughout the year so that they feel appreciated and you keep top-of-mind awareness with them so that when they are ready to do that next design project, they will first think of you.

You can create a referral program and mail it to your customers. When they refer someone to you and you do work with that person, you give your client a gift certificate for their next project with you.

Outrageous Customer Service

I am a proponent of extreme customer service, and I am not alone. In a book called *Outrageous Customer Service* by Scott Gross, the author gives a fascinating but straightforward look at ways to give outrageous customer service. I would suggest that you make customer service a top priority; it is one of the best ways to stand out from the crowd and keep customers. With this type of service, they feel appreciated and know that you care about them. My theory is that we all make mistakes, but it is how we handle the mistakes that sets us apart. Return calls in a timely manner, and take care of problems to the best of your ability as quickly as you can. Go above and beyond, and do the extraordinary; surprise them. Have you ever been in a store where the clerk or employees are too busy talking to each other — or to someone on their cell phone — to stop and wait on you? Have you ever checked into a hotel where the reservation was totally messed up and they would not make it all right? To best make a positive, lasting impression on the customer, they should upgrade you or move you to another hotel at no additional cost to make up for the mistake. How a mistake is handled often determines whether you lose or keep a client. Sometimes, it is a simple as thinking about how you would like to be treated if it happened to you. Read this book and others on customer service so that you can learn to give your customers superior customer service.

Become the Design Expert

We have talked about positioning yourself as an "expert" by hosting seminars. Another way to position yourself is to write design columns for your local newspaper or magazine. Do not get stressed; the articles can be 400 words, and there are an unlimited supply of topics in the world of design that people love to read about. Approach your local TV news programs with the idea of having a small segment on design once a week, or talk to your radio station about hosting a talk show on the weekends. Send a press release out on everything to the local media and offer story ideas. This will also encourage them to contact you for quotes on the design industry.

I write a monthly design column for a regional publication, and I write a monthly column for an industry publication. This gives me credibility as an expert in my field. It also gives me more to put into my portfolio so that when a prospective client sees those articles, they make the connection that I must be an expert.

Public Relations

Write press releases on everything. Here are a couple of Web sites that can give you step-by-step guidance on how to write a good press release:

- **www.wikihow.com/Write-a-Press-Release**
- **www.lunareclipse.net/pressrelease.htm**

Good public relations (PR) can send a positive message to your community about your business. You can create a PR campaign; just have a clear idea of the image you want to portray, and stay focused on that image by defining your goals and creating an effective plan to implement them.

When reaching out to the media, you want to have a clear plan of action and know what they are looking for. The following are some factors that will help you when interacting with the media:

- **Honesty**: The media is looking for honest information from credible sources, so always be truthful and thorough when you write a press release.

- **Respond**: Do not avoid a question if you do not know the answer. Be honest and tell them you do not have that information, but that you can research it and provide it to them in a timely manner. Then you must follow through and get the information to them as quickly as possible.

- **Be precise**: Give a succinct answer, and think about it carefully so that you are not exaggerating or stating something that is not quite true.

- **Follow up**: The media receives stacks of media kits and press releases, so after you have sent something, just follow up to make sure they received it and to see whether they need any more information — but do not bother them too much. Find out how the individual contact prefers to receive information, and send it that way. Most will tell you they prefer e-mail to snail mail.

- **Build a relationship with your contact**: Build a strong relationship with the press, and it will open doors for you. They will contact you for quotes and articles. Also, make it easy for them to write a story by promptly supplying them with everything they need, such as photos and documents if they are requested.

Asking for Referrals

Asking for referrals is a powerful tool, and yet it is something that most people seldom do. Set up a referral program with existing customers, realtors, and other professionals who regularly come into contact with your ideal customer. When you have completed a project for a client, thank them and ask them whether they have a friend who could use your services. Place a message on the bottom of your e-mail about referring someone. Do not be afraid to ask.

Testimonials

Testimonials are one of the most effective, credible marketing tools. Ask clients to write a testimonial letter for you — about you, your work, and the project. Ask them for permission to include it in your portfolio, and portions of it in your advertising. If you can show a before-and-after photo of a room you designed for a client and an accompanying letter of praise from that client, you have credibility.

Take good lines out of a letter and put the quotes in your ads, on your Web site, and in your brochure, and give the name of the client. People feel confident when they see other real people, giving you praise for your services or products.

Cause Marketing

Cause marketing can be a positive and effective way to market your business, gain credibility, network, and give back to your community. Find non-profit events that you believe in, and get involved. Serve on the board of a committee, work on an event, or be a sponsor of an event. By being a sponsor, your logo and name will be included in the promotion of the event; you usually get sign rights at the event; and you will be included in any receptions or parties. Thus, it is hard to go wrong with a credible non-profit in your community.

Portfolio

Show people your work. Have a professional portfolio of photos, preferably before-and-after shots, of projects you have completed. You can stand out from the rest by making your portfolio unique, such as by using a digital picture frame to show your work. Or try taking one beautiful photo of a room you have designed, have it mounted and framed, and bring just that photo with you to show a prospect. Get creative, and find ways to show prospects your work in unique ways.

My final thought for you on this are to make sure you get a professional photo of the room. Architectural photos are difficult, and you do not want to show a prospect an amateur photo. It is worth the investment to pay a professional photographer who is familiar with taking inside and outside building photos so that your work is shown in the best possible light.

CHAPTER 10

So You Have a Sales Lead...
Here is What You Do Next

So, all of your marketing efforts are paying off. Your phone is ringing. In this chapter, we will go over what happens next.

Qualify the Prospect

I strongly encourage you to create a sheet that asks all the qualifying questions you need when you are talking with a prospect. It will save you time and, in the long run, money, if you qualify your prospects. Not everyone will be serious about hiring you, and some may just want to meet with you and take ideas; it is just the nature of the business. Especially with the explosion of HGTV, people are fascinated with design and want to think they can do it themselves. HGTV promotes shows such as *Design on a Dime* and *Trading Spaces*, making the consumer feel that design can be done "on a dime." I strongly suggest qualifying your prospects. The worst-case scenario is that you spend time talking with someone and it will not go any further than that, but the benefits include not wasting time at an appointment and finding out enough information to be prepared for the first meeting. Here are a few questions and ideas to get you started:

- Ask how they heard about you. This question will help you track your marketing efforts.

- Get their address, contact information, and the correct spelling of their name.

- Ask what they need help with. Is it their entire home? Are they remodeling their family room? Do they want window treatments?

- Do they have a budget? Most people will be reluctant to answer this. I usually ask them to give this some thought before our meeting, as it will help me be sure that I show them products and designs that fit within their budget.

- What is their project schedule? Do they want it yesterday, before the holidays, or is the house just being built?

- What is their design style? For example, is it traditional, modern, country, or French country?

- Do they have colors in mind or favorite colors?

This information will help you prepare for your meeting. You will know their budget, what they are looking for, what their style is, what colors they like, and their project schedule. You will also have a better sense of how serious they are about hiring you.

Prepare for the Appointment

Before making the appointment, I usually explain how I work with the prospect during the first contact to make sure they are comfortable with my process. If you give complimentary consultations, be sure to explain what that will include. If you ask for retainers for your work, discuss that and explain what they get for the retainer. Cover whether you work on a project basis or hourly fee, whether you sell product, and any other questions they may have. Discuss how you work with the prospect; if they are comfortable with that, then the next step is to schedule the appointment.

A good way to schedule the appointment without giving the impression that your entire week is open is to offer two days and time ranges, like, "I have Monday the fifth between 1 and 4 p.m., or Wednesday morning available. Which of those days would work best for you?"

Here are some other suggestions that will help you be prepared for a successful appointment:

- Create a client folder and put the information sheet and directions in it.

- Put any promotional material you are going to take with you in the folder.

- Attach a business card to the folder to hand to the client.

- If you have enough information on what the client is looking for and you bring the right fabric books or catalogs, you might be able to sell the client what they want on the first appointment, instead of having to schedule a second appointment.

- Send a follow-up note. A handwritten note goes a long way. Make it short, simple, warm, and professional.

Consultation

You will need to decide whether you will give free consultations or will charge for consultations. If you do not charge, make sure you are clear on what you offer during the consultation. I offer a free consultation, and it includes taking a tour of the client's home, where I will make general suggestions or observations; sitting down to discuss what their design needs, wants, and priorities are; and showing the client my portfolio. If the client wants to move forward, I schedule the next appointment. You will define your own method and procedures. If you charge for the consultation, then you should be prepared to give a little more — perhaps more suggestions than in a "free" consultation.

The Importance of Accurate Measuring

If you are going to do a quote for a client on window coverings, flooring, wallpaper, or furnishing a room, you will want to measure accurately. There are set patterns for measuring windows. Measure from left to right. Measure the inside width and height, the outside (trim to trim) width and height, from top of trim or opening to ceiling and from bottom of trim or opening to the floor — and, finally, you want to know how much room you have on either side of the window.

I measure so that I can give an accurate quote to the client, and if the client approves, I have the person who will install the product also take measurements, and I use their measurements for ordering — whether it is flooring, wallpaper, or window coverings.

Measuring and Pricing of Window Treatments

There are two categories of window coverings: hard and soft. Hard window coverings include roller shades, wooden and faux wood blinds, and shutters. Soft window coverings include panels and top treatments, as well as cornice boards.

There is a process on window coverings that includes:

- Accurately measuring the window
- Doing the correct calculations to determine the final or finished sizes
- Doing accurate fabric yardage calculations

First, measuring the window is crucial. A resource that will help you with treatment styles, how to measure, how to calculate fabric, and terms is the *Encyclopedia of Window Fashions.* They periodically release a new edition, and it is an industry standard go-to book.

When you measure the windows, always measure inside width and height at the top, center, and bottom of the window. This is critical because if you are doing an inside mounted treatment, such as a wooden blind, the window is seldom plum, or the same width or height at each point. Measure the width at the top, center, and bottom, and use the smallest measurement to make certain that your treatment will fit in the window. Then measure the outside measurements — meaning, if the window has trim, you want to measure from the outside of the left side of the trim to the outside of the right side of the trim, and do the same for the outside height — from outside of the top of the trim to the outside of the bottom of the trim. Finally, you need to measure from the outside of the trim to the corner or to any item that might hinder the size of the window treatment on both sides. Then, measure from the outside of the top trim to the ceiling or bottom of crown molding and from the outside of the bottom trim or window ledge to the floor.

These measurements allow you to determine the finished sizes of any type of treatment. For example, if you are doing drapery panels, you might want to install them at the ceiling or at the bottom of the crown molding, as this might give the feeling that the ceilings are higher than they are. You will need to know what the space is from the top of the window to the ceiling to accurately do your calculation for the finished size and for the amount of fabric you will need.

Window treatments will either be an inside or outside mount, meaning that they will either be an inside mount and cover just the glass or the opening itself, or they will be an outside mount or need to cover the opening and frame, if the window is framed. A rule of thumb if you are doing an outside mount of your window treatment is to make sure it completely covers the frame. You do not want to see some of the frame, so outside measurements always include the frames.

Some guidelines you will need to follow for accurate measuring include the following:

- Use measuring tape — steel, wood, or light beam for accuracy.

- Have a set procedure or way you measure; for example, measure around the room from left to right, and measure each window from left to right — then you will always know which window you are talking about, and all windows will be measured the same way.

- If the treatment is on a rod, measure it as well.

- It helps to use the same form each time for each window for consistency.

Drapery Panels

If you are measuring for drapery panels, you will need to take into consideration the stack back. Stack back is the space that is needed for a completely opened or drawn drapery to stack on the wall and clear the opening, making certain the drapery does not obstruct the view. Now you need to determine the finished size and how you want the drapery to be installed. You must allow for the stack back, and you do that by adding one-third times the width measurement.

From there, you need to allow for the overlap and returns. The overlap is the amount the inside or leading edges on each panel overlap each other when the drapery panels are closed. Returns are the amount of the drapery panel that wraps around the end of the rod to the wall. The average return is 3 ½ inches, so you would need to add 3 ½ inches + 3 ½ inches = 7 inches so that you include the end of the rod on both sides. When you have a layered treatment such as a valance, panels, and sheers, you would allow 3 ½ inches on either side for the first layer, the sheers, then 5 ½ inches for the drapery panels, and finally, a 7 ½-inch return on the valance or top treatment so that all three treatments fit correctly on the window.

When you measure for the length or height of the drapery panels, you do your measurements as outlined above. There is an allowance for the bottom, called a pull-up. Allow one inch for the pull-up. Determine what type of rod you will be using, if there is a rod pocket and if there is a header. The size of the rod will determine the size of the rod pocket, and you can decide what length you want a header, if your design includes one. There are traverse rods, which allow you to hang pleated drapery on cartridges, and they move in and out to open and close the drapery. There are decorative wooden and iron drapery rods, and you might use a rod pocket, clips, or rings on this type of rod. There are also heavy oval rods that are not seen and are usually used with a rod pocket treatment.

Example:
Window opening length. . . . . 75"
Adjustment for placing the rod above the frame of the window . . .plus 4"
Allow for the header. . . . . .plus 2"

From bottom of window to the floor . . . . .plus 8"

Finished length. . . . . equals 89"

Draperies can be just below the sill, to the floor, or can puddle on the floor. You can place them right above the window opening or trim, higher on the wall, or even to the ceiling, depending on your design and what the treatment is designed to contribute to the room. You must also consider the fullness factor of the treatment. If you want the panel to be flat, reflecting just the actual width of the treatment, you would use a 1 fullness; however, typically a 2 ½ is used to give a fuller look to the treatment, and because of the lightness of sheer fabric, often a 3X fullness factor is used.

There are many types of soft treatments. The current trend tends to lean toward more casual and clean treatments instead of heavy, ornate treatments. Roman shades and clean-lined valances are examples of the clean-line, casual look. Swags and cascades are more traditional, heavier valance top treatments that are often seen in formal designs.

There are different measurement methods for each type of treatment, and you will need to either have a college class or some type of seminar or training classes on understanding how to measure for each type of treatment and calculate the amount of fabric and material you will need to create your treatment. This will affect not only the accuracy of the treatment, but your cost, as well. If you underestimate the amount of fabric, you might have to order additional fabric. Fabric comes in dye lots, and when you get the same fabric from a different dye lot, you run the high risk of the colors being off. You would then have to re-order the full amount of needed fabric, and this could wipe out your profit. You want to be extremely careful and accurate with all your measurements and calculations on fabric.

Representative list of different top treatments:

- Pleated valance
- Box pleat
- Inverted box pleat
- Balloon valance
- Austrian valance

These are just a few styles and, of course, you can design your own custom valances.

There are fabric companies that make it easy for you if you use their basic designs. Carole Fabrics and Kasmir Fabrics both offer good deals: They offer, let us say, a dozen designs. They also sell fabric. They give you a matrix that allows you to choose one of their fabric patterns and one of their designs, and based on the finished width (FW) and finished length (FL), they give you a price. No fabric calculation is needed because the price includes the labor and the fabric. These companies are good for specific projects, but I recommend you find a local workroom that you can work with — someone whom you trust and agree with. You must also like their work.

A workroom is critical to your success. They must know what they are doing, complete projects when they say they will, and be professional. They might occasionally be in front of your customers, and you want to make sure that they are not working retail or directly with the end client, as this could be a conflict of interest. The other person you need to find who is critical to your success is a professional window treatment installer. The installer will always be in front of the client, so they must not discuss prices or you with the client. They need to understand how to measure and how to install whatever treatment you design. They will need the appropriate tools and will need to be neat and clean, as they will be in your clients' homes. It does not hurt for you to have your own tool kit that you always

Before

Photographs provided by Jane Speroff

After

bring with you. It could include fabric scissors, pins, measuring tape, a drill, and a level. You will find that you might accumulate stray brackets, rings, and screws as well.

It is important to understand how to calculate fabric yardage. There are three basic elements in calculating the yardage: the width of the material, the cut length, and dividing by 36. So, the width of the fabric multiplied by your cut length divided by 36 plus number of yards of fabric. This is one of many formulas you will need to know when calculating your yardage. If you find a good workroom, they will work with you on learning these calculations.

Wall Covering

Wallpaper comes in different sizes. The standard American roll will be 18 to 36 inches wide, and the length can run from 12 to 24 feet. There are also Euro rolls that come in metric measurements. Wallpaper is priced by the single roll, although it is typically sold in double rolls; be aware of this when you are working on your pricing.

There are many types of wallpaper. Foil paper has a metallic look to the front of it and a thin sheet of metal on the fabric back. Grass cloth is actual natural grass that is woven and glued onto paper backing. There is fabric-backed vinyl wall covering that is durable, scrubable, and strippable. Wallpaper designs will sometimes have a repeat, which is where the pattern repeats and how those repeats match up when installing the paper.

Measuring is fairly straightforward. You can use graph paper to do a rough sketch of the room and note any openings, such as doors, windows, and fireplaces. You will measure the width of each wall and the height of each wall from floor to ceiling and add those numbers together. Next, you need to determine your total square feet by multiplying the height of the ceiling by the length of the wall. To determine how much wallpaper you will need, know whether you are working with American rolls or Euro rolls. If you are working with American rolls, you will divide the total square footage of the space by 30 to get the number of single rolls you will need for the job. Professional paper hangers will deduct for the openings, but it never hurts to have extra just in case, so if you do not have huge openings, you might want to consider not doing any deductions for the openings.

You might want to have your wallpaper hanger do the measuring for you, and when you have selected the paper, you can calculate how much of the paper you need.

Flooring

There is quite a bit to know about flooring. There is carpeting, hardwood flooring, laminate flooring, and stone. I recommend you find seminars at market and from suppliers on the different types of flooring and how to measure for them. You can also have your floor installers measure for you.

Pricing and Estimating

One way to determine an hourly fee is to find out what other designers are charging in your region. The hourly rates of designers range from $60 per hour to $300, depending on geographic location and level of expertise. Designers often decide on these hourly rates by adding all their expenses up and then dividing the billable hours that they can bill clients directly. Billable hours are hours you can bill clients for your services directly, while non-billable hours are the time spent doing research, setting up meeting rooms, and doing general business work, such as paying bills. Hourly rates should include meeting time, research, design, illustration, quality control, revisions, clerical work, client service, and proposals.

Another way to establish your hourly rate is by multiplying all the salaries you pay by three. If you are the only person who works at your business, and you make $40,000 a year, multiply $40,000 x 3, which equals $120,000. You can count a third of the business as overhead, another third as salary, and the final third as profits for your business. The total of your salary would be $40,000 per year. Now divide the salary by the number of weeks you work to get a weekly salary. Estimate the number of hours and divide this into the weekly salary. This will give you your hourly fee to charge. This formula works well for small businesses.

Cost plus is another method of payment for designers. The designer is paid to design, but also paid to purchase the goods that go into the project on a cost-plus basis. There are usually markups on all charges of freight and delivery.

Some firms handle the prices as fee-based. A fixed rate or fee is when the designer and client agree on a single fee that includes all the work done. Often, this type of arrangement has a schedule of payments the client will make to meet the total. A set price is established based on the number of hours, or even square footage. The price is often paid in increments.

Square footage is another method some interior designers use to price jobs. The price is based on the number of square feet the room or rooms have. This can be a difficult method because some homes will require more work and time than others. You may lose money when time could be spent on other, more lucrative projects.

Project Estimates

You will be doing many estimates, and estimates involve plenty of number crunching.

An estimate is like a blueprint of a project. Some estimates are itemized item by item, and others reflect a total price for the project. Most designers at some time must do both.

Estimates can become contracts if they are done with enough detail. Sometimes, clients have a project in mind and want an estimate to get a price range on the cost. When doing a preliminary estimate, always explain your fees and costs to the client so they understand them. Estimates are an important part of the design business.

When preparing an estimate for clients, keep these basic guidelines in mind. Who is the client you are preparing the estimate for? What type of estimate is it? Always give a name and general description of the project. After this, give a detailed description of the project or overview. For example, for a kitchen and bathroom-remodeling job, describe who will design the project and handle the interior work, what equipment is used, what merchandise is needed, and what the overall costs are. You will need a concise description of the client project and whether it needs to be done in phases. The responsibilities of the designer and subcontractors should be spelled out in detail. The suppliers, merchandise, and equipment needed for the job should be included.

Estimates can include photography and art supply fees, special expertise for dealing with walls and ceilings, zoning, wall treatments, millworks, window treatments, furnishings, accessories, appliances, delivery and costs of merchandise, payment terms, and other charges.

The estimate should include a detailed description of the project based on the client meeting. You might visit the site, take measurements, and write detailed notes about the research needed. You might want to mention whether you will need detailed schematics for the project and what the client's budget is. What will they need for the interior of the room? Will they need furniture, paint, rugs, new walls, appliances, and floors? This should be written in the estimate. The designers and contractors working on the project should be listed with costs. This is usually considered the project development phase.

Next, the estimate will include the scope of the project or details about the design of the project or design development. Some projects are broken into different phases with information on each phase written in the estimate. Development phases would include site schematics or drawings.

When the project is implemented, you will need a list all materials ordered or purchased. It can include wall fabrics and finishing, different types of flooring or ceiling materials, assorted fixtures and hardware, furniture, custom orders for special projects, lighting fixtures, appliances, cabinets, and accessories. Estimate forms can be customized to the individual type of business that you run so it is easy to fill out and does not have unnecessary information. It should have information about the construction site personnel and the project schedule.

Retainer

Working with a retainer is a personal decision that you will want to give some serious thought. Will you primarily be consulting and working at an hourly rate, or will you be creating proposals and presentations and selling product? Perhaps you work on a project basis, so you give the client a total project price. You might consider charging a retainer to cover your time in researching, designing, pricing, and preparing the proposal for your next meeting. Most people who are serious about working with you will be willing to pay a small retainer with the explanation of paying for your time. Of course, if you receive a retainer for designing window coverings, and the client decides not to purchase, are you prepared to give them the designs? Many people are completely unaware of the amount of time that goes into designing and creating presentations and proposals. Asking for a retainer gives you the opportunity to show them the benefit of working with you by describing what goes into working on a project.

Research, Design, and Proposal

You will develop your own process for this part of the job. The scope of the job itself will tell you whether you will be coming back to the client with a few fabric samples or a full-blown design board with furniture, window coverings, furniture, and everything else the project encompasses. Some designers will not do design boards without being compensated for the time and cost involved, while others will give a full presentation but will not leave the samples or ideas behind unless the client approves the project. When you are just starting out, it might be beneficial to be willing to do the full presentation when you feel the prospect is serious.

Prepare for the Presentation

Clients need plenty of visuals. So, for example, if you have designed custom window coverings for them, sketch the design, bring a memo sample or sample book of the fabric, and give them a written proposal. You might need to create a floor plan of a room with furniture placement or sketch a rendering of your ideas. This can be presented informally or on a presentation board. Also, listen to the client and adapt to them. For example, I met with a young military officer who had purchased his first condo. After our first meeting, I knew that I needed to speak his language and let him know that I understood him. He presented *me* with a PowerPoint presentation of what he wanted and what his budget was. So, I came back to him with a PowerPoint presentation that had a photo of each piece of furniture, a sketch of each window treatment, a photo of each accessory, and a suggested furniture placement sketch with a total project price.

He was thrilled and signed the contract the day I made the presentation. We then communicated almost exclusively via e-mail. This was the best way to reach him. Other people may never touch a computer, so I would never do a PowerPoint for them. When you are meeting with a prospect for the consultation, listen to them, watch them, and learn how they like to interact.

The Upsell

To up sell is to increase the sell by enticing the customer to purchase upgraded products or additional products, like accessories. I know many designers who keep inventory of just accessories, and when they design an entire room for a client, they select accessories that will finish off the room and place them in the room for the client to see. Often, this simple act can increase a sale by hundreds, or even thousands, of dollars.

You might upsell a client with an upgraded seat cushion on the sofa, beadtrim on their valance for the window, or by adding a top window treatment to a window where they originally requested a shade only. Point out the value and reasons why these items would enhance their design and you can often increase the sale.

Client Appointment and Presentation

During a presentation appointment, do not leave item numbers or information on the products you have presented that will allow the client to "shop" you. Sadly, this happens often, and with the Internet, it is easy. There are customers who genuinely want your assistance and want to pay you for your time, knowledge, and products, and others who want the best price and want to take your information and shop it around for the best price. Protect yourself as best you can from people who just want your knowledge, and do not want to pay for it.

Contract

I would advise you to take some time and decide what information you need in a contract. If you can get your hands on a competitor's contract, you can see what they do. You can also consult with your attorney and have them draw up a contract for you. The following are some suggestions of information to include in your contract:

- Your name and contact information
- The client's name and contact information
- The scope of the work, including a listing of products
- Sub-total
- Sales tax, if applicable
- Total contract amount
- Any deductions, such as for gift certificates or special discounts
- Amount of deposit
- Amount that will be due upon installation

There are many other legal items that need to be addressed, and your attorney can assist you with this information.

CHAPTER 11

Congratulations! You Got the Project...Now What?

You got the project; now the real work begins. You will be placing orders, coordinating delivery, supervising fabrication of products, and directing the install. At this stage, you have worked hard to get this approval. Now you want to focus on getting the ball in motion and making sure everything is correct so that you do not lose time, money, or a client with a mistake.

Deposit

It is important to get at least a 50 percent deposit from clients when they approve the project and sign the contract. You may decide, on a large project, to also ask for draws along the way; if you do, make certain that is spelled out in the contract with the date and amount of each draw.

Thank-You Note

A follow-up thank-you note is a personal touch. It is the least you can do to immediately thank customers for their business. You can purchase an off-the-shelf thank-you card that fits the client and situation, or you might have personal note cards with your name or company name printed on them. Either way you go, a hand-written, heartfelt thank-you will instill goodwill with your customer.

Placing Orders with Vendors

You will want to get orders placed as soon as possible. Custom furnishings can take as long as 12 weeks to be fabricated, and if you are sending COM (customers' own fabric) instead of using one of the manufacturer's fabrics, you will need to order the fabric and have it drop-shipped to the manufacturer before they can even process the order. Along the way, you will want to stay in touch and follow-up on the status of the fabric and furniture. There might be window coverings to order, and again, you will have to order the fabric, lining, and trim, have it shipped to your workroom, and create work orders to be sent to the workroom.

If you are using accounting software such as QuickBooks, you can use the purchase order they give you. You can also purchase blank purchase order forms at the office supply store and handwrite the orders. Use the customer's last name as the side mark for all of the parts of their project so that you and the suppliers can track the orders.

Tracking Orders

Some businesses call this aspect of the business "traffic" because you are keeping track of where each order is in the process.

- Order the fabrics

- Confirm they were delivered

- Confirm furniture is in production

- Confirm workroom received materials and their schedule on fabricating the window treatments

- Confirm when the items are given to the freight companies and when they are delivered to the receiver

Coordinating Deliveries and Installations

It will be up to you to coordinate the delivery and installation on your projects with the vendors. I recommend sending your receiver a purchase order of sorts that tells them what pieces to expect, from what vendor, and an estimated delivery date. Do not just take whatever freight company the vendor uses if you have one that you like to use. You will want to make it clear on the purchase order to the vendor which freight company to use, and let the receiver know this as well.

Finding a good receiver, good installers, and good freight companies can save your business. They reflect on you; if they mess up, it is your problem. The client looks to you for a seamless project. Do your research and find out who the installers and receivers are in the area that other designers are using. Interview them, and find out what they charge and how they work. Communicate as much information as possible to them about the project.

I suggest that you always be on-site for installations and deliveries. That way, you are there in case any problems arise and can give directions on how to resolve the issues. Also, the client will not feel compelled to talk to the installer about any concerns or ask about pricing or any other things that you would not want discussed with the people that you have hired. You need to have a clear understanding up-front with anyone you hire to work on your projects: They work for you; they should be professional and courteous with your customers; and they should never discuss costs or issues with the client. You want to show the client that you are there to take care of them during the installation, and finally, you want to be there to do the walk-through with them and collect your final payment.

Keeping in Touch with Your Customer

The client has no idea what it takes on the back end to do what you do. They are more familiar with HGTV, where in a half hour, a room magically gets decorated. Therefore, even though you tell them it will be eight to ten weeks, it is a good idea to call every now and then and give them an update and let them know whether there are any delays or other issues. It will make them feel like you are on top of the project and keeping them in the loop, and it will give them additional attention.

Follow Up After Installation

It cost less to keep an existing client than it does to go out and get a new client, and there are little things you can do that help you keep an existing client.

Suppose you have completed the install and it went well. You have thanked the clients, they are happy, and you have been paid. Many designers will have a gift at installation or bring it by shortly after the installation. You can get creative with this. If it was a large project, it might justify a larger gift. It is a thank-you gift. Do not make it a promo item with your logo on it; make it personal. For instance, if your client is an avid wine drinker and you know she likes Italian wines, you might buy a special bottle of a good Italian wine and put it in a beautiful wine bag as a gift. Another idea is if the clients purchased window treatments, you could have the workroom make throw pillows for the sofa that matches or coordinates with the window coverings and give them to the clients as a thank-you gift. It does not necessarily have to cost much, but the thought goes a long way. It lets the clients know that you appreciate them and their business, and that you took the time to give them a personalized thank-you gift.

CHAPTER 12

Current Trends in Design

Outdoor Living

There has been a growing trend to create outdoor living spaces, especially in areas that have tropical climates. The increase in homes with outdoor kitchens is significant. Also, outdoor living areas around pools are quite popular, and there has been an explosion of new products that are designed for outdoor use, from furniture to fabrics for window treatments.

Color Trends

Color trends change annually. The Color Marketing Group (CMG) and Pantone are just two of the groups that predict color trends in a variety of products — not just design products. You can stay on top of these trends by attending market, subscribing to industry publications, and meeting with vendor reps.

For example, for 2009, Pantone announced its color of the year as mimosa. Knowing this gives you something to share with your clients and lets them know that you are on top of the current trends. They may never have mimosa-colored walls, but they will feel good that their designer is up-to-date on the latest color trends.

Luxury Kitchen Design

The trends show that luxury kitchen design is increasing. Baby boomers and retirees want their dream kitchen. It may be the last kitchen they design, so they want the best, newest, greatest products, design, and gadgets.

Induction cooking has made a comeback and is showing up in luxury kitchen design. Today, there has been a move back to aluminum inserts inside stainless steel pans, and induction cooking is part of the luxury kitchen design.

Kitchen trends have gone through changes. In the 1980s, styles had a hard, industrial look that was reflected in the flooring. During the 1990s, the Old World look was the hot trend for kitchens, but now it is waning in popularity. The French country style is still popular and has seen a few changes. Globally, the traditional style is softening, but is still in strong demand in the United States.

The contemporary look is changing, with softer edges mixed with natural materials, and an integration of woods with harder materials, like a granite countertop with maple wood. There is a large American influence in kitchen designs around the world, but Italian manufacturers lead in the new luxury designs. Contemporary design does not have to mean cold and sparse, however; the new contemporary style includes softer edges, natural products with clean lines, and an uncluttered look. It might include stainless-steel appliances and stainless-steel countertops. Furniture-looking elements versus the box cabinets are popular. The contemporary-styled kitchens have a seamless look, integrating cabinets that disguise the refrigerator, and faucets that disappear. Wine storage units are also becoming quite popular in the new kitchen designs.

The other news in luxury kitchen design is the amazing products being designed, including everything from water faucets that show you the temperature — red when the water is hot and blue when it is cold — to faucets that fold down and disappear into the cabinetry. KWC offers two versions of Pure Jet — a regular faucet and pull-out plus a pure water filtration system. In Europe, there is a product that produces sparkling water, which needs a cartridge and can be designed as part of the faucet or a stand-alone part.

Energy-efficient appliances are eco-friendly and part of the latest trends. There are so many options to consider when selecting appliances. Of course, you have the basics like the refrigerator, stove, dishwasher, and microwave, but above and beyond those, you might look at a wine cooler, or an espresso or deluxe cappuccino maker. Even the basic appliances will take research to make a selection: electric or gas stove? In regard to the refrigerator, you have many options of finishes, including the traditional white, black, and stainless steel, but you also can choose from colors like blue or red. If a red fridge is too much for your client but he or she wants to add a splash of color, consider a Kitchen Aid® stand mixer, where you have color choices including Reef Blue, Plum, or Empire Red.

The following are examples of some of the different countertop materials.

Granite: It is an igneous rock, which means it was once molten and formed as it cooled deep within the earth. Granite has different minerals in it that you see as flecks and specks throughout the stone. Some granite may have veining, which is similar to marble. Granite is hard and durable and is almost impossible to scratch. You will want to seal the granite and probably re-seal it every one to two years. Granite can be polished and shiny, and is not very porous, which makes it easy to clean.

Quartz: Man-made, this engineered stone is non-porous. It never has to be sealed or polished, and it is durable and resistant to spills; however, it can be damaged by high heat. It is much heavier than granite, and you can find it by brand names that include Silestone™ and Cambria.

Marble: Used for many years for countertops, marble can stain easily; some experts think it is too soft for use as a countertop, but it is beautiful and is found in many kitchens.

Solid surface: Man-made, it can be an acrylic or plastic material colored by resins. They have a consistent pattern and color.

Concrete: It has become a popular choice, partly because it can be poured and molded into any shape you can imagine. You will need to apply layers of sealant.

Back splashes: This might include slate, glass tiles, or stainless steel.

Wall Covering

This trend has been exploding in Europe and is slowly making its way to America. Americans have the image of the old, hard-to-remove wallpaper of our mothers' generation. However, the new wallpaper is easy to remove, easy to clean, and comes in an array of wonderful patterns, colors, and textures. Wallpaper for an entire room might be too much for your client, but you could use wallpaper on an accent wall. It is worth considering wallpaper when you are designing, as it gives you more options to choose from to complete a room.

Faux Painting

How often do you see a faux finish? The next time you are in a public building, a commercial office, or your neighbor's home, take a good look at the walls, the floor, the ceiling, the trim, and even the furniture. You might be surprised by what you see.

A professional faux painter can add a beautiful custom touch of art to a room. An accent wall in one room, the ceiling in the dining room, and perhaps the entire guest bath in a faux treatment can unleash a unique style in the home. There are some truly beautiful techniques that can be spectacular. One of my favorites is the Old World plaster look. It is sometimes called aged wall plaster, which means old plaster painted with lime wash and tinted with earth colors.

The best examples of authentic aged walls can be found in Venice and Tuscany in Italy, where you can find walls that were color-washed decades ago and have naturally weathered. The colors have faded in the sun, and you sometimes see brick that might be exposed. Creating this look takes skill, which is why you want to hire a professional faux artist to create this Old World look for you. This style looks wonderful with the Mediterranean and Tuscan styles that are popular today. If you are looking for a casual beach style, the linen technique can create the feeling of a casual beach cottage on the ocean with carefully chosen colors.

Decorative faux painting as we know it has seen a resurgence that began in the early 1990s. This is perhaps due to somewhat of a rebellion to wallpaper, which was difficult to apply and even more difficult to remove. Faux finishing is not new, however; it has been around for a long time.

Although faux finishing can technically be traced back to the walls of the cave man, we need only look back to the Renaissance for the faux finishing that shaped the current trend. During this time, artists were commissioned by wealthy patrons to create beautiful spaces by artfully applying color and images. Faux artists would paint faux marble, faux wood, faux stone, decorative architectural elements, and Trompe l'oeil Murals. Trompe l'oeil, pronounced "tromp lowel," is French and means "to fool or deceive the eye." It takes great talent and skill to achieve a realistic look.

Another option is tortoise shelling. If you use it over a large surface, it can have a look of sophistication — and it is quite striking. This technique goes back to Roman times, when turtle shells were imported to Europe from the Far East. As the shells became expensive and increasingly difficult to obtain, the artists of the time developed a technique to create a faux look for the shell. The Pompeii Fresco is one such beautiful work of art.

Out of Europe came two distinct styles. The Italian style was realistic but not exact, as it was, by design, created to be viewed at a distance. The French style evolved with intricate, complicated techniques with the goal of creating finishes that could be scrutinized up close.

Faux gained favor again and again during the neoclassical nineteenth century and the Art Deco era of the 1920s. It was frequently used in commercial buildings; however, in the 1990s resurgence, it became popular in home environments. Today, it is wildly popular, from the do-it-yourself classes you can take at Home Depot^{SM} to the true artist.

Whether it is an accent wall, kitchen cabinets, a piece of furniture, or an entire room, a talented faux artist can transform your home into an Italian Piazza or a formal, elegant room with marble walls or columns.

Design for Aging Baby Boomers

The aging baby boomers population will create many opportunities for designers to create homes and living quarters for them. This runs from retirement communities, assisted living centers, nursing homes, condos, and regular homes, to recreation and medical faculties.

Some of the new design trends in health care facilities include more natural light that comes into the interior rooms. The faculties are being designed with more open space on walkways, and the interior is designed for noise reductions. Some buildings have healing gardens, therapeutic art and sculpture, digital and wireless communications, and Internet access. Many college campuses are designing new programs and buildings to attract the senior market. Wellness centers connected to senior communities are being designed that help them with diet, exercise, intellectual, health, and other issues.

Principles to keep in mind when designing for boomers are to design or create a home-like atmosphere and avoid the institutional look. Depending on the project and budget, it may need to be economical and easy to maintain. Strive to create areas that give seniors a chance to be creative and active. Learn about the special types of products and merchandise geared to seniors by contacting suppliers and vendors in your region.

Senior living designers will need to learn to design for seniors by providing buildings that promote mental and physical wellness. Designs to increase people's participation in activities, whether in groups or alone, will be important. Many clients, when asked in a survey what was important in senior housing design, rated exercise rooms, computer equipment, game rooms, physical and occupational therapy areas, beauty parlors, and libraries as priorities. New types of programs or facilities being added to buildings for seniors are spas, refreshment areas, indoor pools, locker rooms, whirlpools, therapy rooms, walking paths, and computer rooms. The senior of today is more physically and mentally active than ever before.

Technology is important to the design of senior living environments. Technology that lets caregivers monitor an elderly relative from a long distance is one option. Small, wireless motion sensors are put in seniors' living quarters. Changes are communicated through e-mail, text message, and cell phone. There are computer-assisted devices that help the elderly with memory and intellectual problems and monitor at-home health conditions electronically. More designers for the elderly will be using technology as part of their overall design.

The bathroom design for seniors often comes with safety issues. Ella's Bubbles (**www.ellasbubbles.com**) offers a walk-in tub designed for seniors, in which the tub has an airtight door seal that prevents water from spilling onto the floor outside the tub. Some tubs have lifts that lower the person into the tub when it is full. These are called safety tubs. Installing grab bars near toilets and bathtubs is also often helpful to the elderly. Another product to consider is non-slip floors, in which you add a coating to tile or marble floors that does not hurt the finish. Safety is important for all clients, but especially for the elderly. Each bathroom designed should be suited to the group it serves.

When designing for the elderly in the kitchen, remember to make the area more accessible and easy to use. Using rolling carts for storage and easy moving is one idea. Lever faucets are often easier to grab and use in the sink, as are spray attachments. Self-cleaning stoves and pull-out shelves to put pots on so you do not carry them long distances are also helpful. Side-by-side refrigerators are easier to open, as are bottom freezer models. Pull-out shelves and counters at different heights for easier use are new trends in kitchens for seniors. Shallow sink bowls that allow room for knees for seated users are popular. Some sinks have levers or no touch or infrared controls. And oven doors that open sideways may work better for some elderly. Newer faucets that have fiber-optic threads that turn the water red when it is hot and blue when it is cold help seniors whose touch sensitivity for hot and cold are diminished.

Good lighting and heated floors are similarly often helpful. Lighting should add to visual orientation and safety. Placement of light switches at easy-to-reach levels is important for proper use. Wall-mounted ovens are easier to use than ranges for older seniors. On cabinets, think of removing doors or replacing them with glass so you can see everything in them. Lower the height of wall cabinets in the kitchen so they are easier to use and reach.

CHAPTER 13

Green Design

Green design, including eco-friendly products, is becoming more important in the world of design. From home kitchens and baths to green commercial office buildings, green design is in. The industry of design has long been conscious of going green when possible. With an increase in energy conservation and environmental awareness, more products are being offered than ever before to the consumer. With the move toward green design, you might consider specializing in green, eco-friendly design work.

Green office buildings can be designed with more environmental healthy materials, thus improving the health of employees. Salvage products that can be reused, instead of making new ones, are also green building materials — these can include bricks, lumber, plumbing, and fixtures. Green products are countertops and flooring made from recycled materials that give off no volatile organic compounds (VOCs). Bamboo, cork, and linoleum are considered green flooring. Water-efficient appliances that conserve and use less water are also considered green.

Lighting is another area where green rules. Solid-state lighting is a bulb or lamp that uses the movement of electrons through a semiconductor to generate light. The semiconductor is a solid block. There is no filament that heats up and burns out, so it is a much more efficient light. It can last up to ten times longer than regular bulbs and contains no harmful mercury, like some light bulbs.

Paint is now made with lower levels of VOCs, which are solvents that are released into the air as paint dries. They can cause headaches and dizziness. Many companies now make paints that are lower in VOCs, and consumers and designers alike who wish to design green appreciate these paints.

If you do not need a large oven or refrigerator, use a smaller one to save more energy. Some companies make cabinets that are free of formaldehyde, which is a toxic gas, and others made of particleboard or 75-percent recycled or recovered material. Solar panels for heating are another way to save on energy in some homes. Electric walk-behind mowers save on gas, which are designed for small properties, but are not well-suited to large areas. Using bamboo as a raw material in kitchens is gaining in popularity. It is one of the fastest-growing plants in the world and requires little water or fertilizer for harvesting. Bronze, copper, and stone are gaining in popularity for kitchens and bathrooms.

Kitchens can be designed to be environmentally friendly while still having style and not breaking your client's budget. Replacing incandescent light bulbs with compact fluorescents and installing a dimmer switch on light fixtures are ways to conserve energy. Appliances that bear the Energy Star® labels use less water and energy than the standard models. Kitchen faucets that offer cold, hot, and filtered water from the same spout help conserve water. Green kitchen designs strive for simplicity, and lately, woods like cherry and oak are fashionable for cabinets and trims. Many companies are designing energy-efficient products from light bulbs to kitchen appliances.

Furthermore, furniture made of bamboo is growing in popularity. A hollow dining chair made of bamboo is strong and functional. Furniture made of aspen and yellow poplar seeks to eliminate wood waste. Wall textures made of coconut palms that would have normally been destroyed create an interesting texture for walls and are eco-friendly. Vinyl tiles in unusual shapes and colors make interesting patterns on the kitchen floor and bathroom.

And many manufacturers make tile, carpeting, flooring, textiles, or fabrics from materials that are environmentally friendly. They strive to offer consumers products that are safer and better for the environment. Some flooring can be made of linseed oil from flax, pine rosin, wood and cork flour, limestone, and pigments. Today, floors are sometimes now made of cork, but only the bark of the cork oak tree is used, as a cork tree can live from 150 to 200 years. Some manufacturers use recycled cork from wine bottles. Cork furniture and accessory products have shown up recently at market showrooms, as well as in creative, environmentally friendly furnishings. Countertops made of these woods are environmentally sound. Some countertops are even made with recycled glass.

Bathrooms are now becoming greener. Some have products that use formaldehyde-free wood and low-VOC paint. The vanities for the bathroom are made of this material. Bathroom toilets are being equipped with new flushing technology. For some, you can select the water flow depending on what you are flushing, which can decrease water usage.

Solar products, which use the sun's energy, are gaining in popularity. Solar skylights transfer energy from the sun into your home and they are less expensive than ordinary skylights. Sustainability of products is a big trend in green design. It means a product that is good for the environment and wears well or is durable. It does not break down over time and harm the environment, but enhances or improves the environment. Some companies take this goal seriously and have product databases that list their products with properties, environmental factors, and certifications. Such companies focus on carbon, climate, recycling, greenhouse gas, energy conservation, and other issues.

Green building design can have positive impacts on the environment. Designing smaller homes can save on building materials, and they are also more energy efficient. Using green design in buildings has reduced the amount of waste disposal used in construction, and they are often better designed, resulting in fewer repairs and better quality material that lasts longer. Many green building designs can reduce soil erosion and water runoff.

Consumers are also recently returning to smaller furniture. Fabric made from recycled polyester is a colorful, vibrant new product. Also, green furniture is stylish and good for the environment, with certified-sustainable wood, recycle plastic, or metal. It is furniture that is durable, flexible, and has low toxicity.

Designers continue to see a trend in finding ways to incorporate outside design within the entire home. There will be increased customization of furniture, whether clients restore antique furniture in the family or go out and buy it new. With the help of technology, you can take any image and make it into a wall or floor covering. This is a trend of combining traditional crafts with new technology and an interest in textures and materials.

Leather is coming back as a popular material for sofas and chairs. Consumers care about materials, so designers must know this aspect well — even if they do not specialize in green design. Wall murals will become popular with some consumers, so designers may have to design custom murals for clients who want one to suit their personality. Elegance will be important, but at lower costs. Recycling and reusing products will become more common than ever before.

In hospitality, trends for holistic hotels and resorts are coming into fashion. These properties use thermal heat and nontoxic building materials and emphasize green principles and environmentally healthy concepts for hotel guests. Some spas incorporate the healing of body and mind into their vacation experience for customers. This uses both the popular green design concept and the holistic concept that goes along with this. Hotels look at social, community, environmental, and financial factors when they design new buildings. Often, non-toxic building materials are used with flooring with radiant heat and cooling.

Many hotels are designed with escapism in mind. The tourist is coming to escape problems at home or change their environment. It is less common for hotels to just have business guests. Often, they have people who want to address their business and enjoy the time they spend while they are there. Bathrooms in hotel guest rooms are an important part of the stay. A good showerhead that provides a pulsating spray seems to rate big with many hotel guests. And some designers are seeing guests who are interested in staying at hotels that observe green design principles.

Some hospitality companies prefer green design, so it is important to be prepared. For example, the Hyatt Regency® in Denver, Colorado, has a recycling program that has greatly reduced landfill waste. Some hotels have installed solar panels to save energy. Clearly, green design can pertain to every specialty in interior design.

Basic Guidelines for Designers

You may want to thoroughly examine the green trend for environmentally safe products. It is growing and will continue to be an important issue in years to come. Before you jump in, you should consider whether you are suited to this area. And once you decide you want to go green, you will need a business plan. How will you incorporate green design into your business? You may want to interview interior designers who have green firms to see what they are doing to achieve their goals. This may be as simple as researching green vendors, contacting them to see what their products are like, and then ordering them if customers want them.

For example, paint with low VOCs is one product you might want to offer customers. Perhaps if you build houses, you might want to offer solar panels for energy conservation on the roof for the customers who are interested in purchasing such products. You may want to use more recycled products or cut down on products that have contaminants.

When you work on an interior design project, research products you might use that are green. Look for products that might be recycled or salvaged and save energy. There are many vendors for green furniture, building supplies, paint, and other accessories. Begin by researching local companies that may supply some products. Consider using antique and collectible items in an effort to recycle. Try to find vendors who use traditional materials in building and may have some green products to offer if you cannot find any green vendors in your area.

Sunlight, Wind, and Water

Sunlight is an important energy source used in green design. It can be harnessed to heat and light the home. Using solar power in a design project means observing where the sunlight falls during the day, in the home, and on the site. Do you have more sun than shade in the home or building? Where is it located, and what is the climate? Sunlight intensity varies with season, climate, and time of the day. Light in a room decreases your need for electricity and saves on energy. New window technology increases the use of sun in your home and decreases the presence of UV rays.

The general rule is if glass or windows are equal to about 5 percent of the room's floor area, then you receive enough sunlight. Placing windows on at least two walls of any room usually provides balanced lighting. Windows are a good way to improve the sunlight use in a room; you can find ways to use the energy of the sun naturally. Paint rooms a light color to reflect the light and outside. Skylights are good for bringing light into dark rooms, but they can bring problems if not installed properly. Some problems include heat loss, overheating in the summer, and leaking water into the house.

Passive solar heating means a home or room is designed to use the sun's energy effectively. Letting light in during winter through south-facing windows is one way to utilize this method.

Thermal mass means selecting building materials when you design a room that are good for natural heating and cooling. The materials work with your design to be effective. You want to place materials where the sun hits during the day.

Many simple techniques can improve your use of solar energy. Shading devices, like awnings or trellises, can be put above windows to help reduce heat. Whether you need more sun or less, adding and removing windows is an option. Heating your water with the sun is now possible with solar-powered water heaters.

In most regions, if the glass area of the windows is at least 5 percent of the floor area, it should provided adequate light for basic vision. North-facing windows often create the best light and the least amount of glare. Map out the use of sunlight by observing how the space uses this type of energy. The power of observation goes a long way toward finding solutions to lighting problems.

In Washington, D.C., the government passed a bill in 2006 to design more energy-efficient buildings. Some of the elements of green design include water-free urinals, solar panels for buildings, and using building materials that reduce waste and conserve water. Certified green buildings are known to save from 20 to 50 percent on energy costs. The U.S. Green Building Council is involved in this project.

As a green designer, you may be dealing with air quality in a home as part of your design work. Air often moves quickly, giving it power and force. As a designer, think about the direction the wind blows on the site you are designing. Turbine ventilators, which are often put on rooftops, are run by the breezes or wind that makes them spin. This allows cooler air to enter the home at lower levels, replaced by exhausted air. Ceiling fans help with natural ventilation. Use the fan to cool the house in summer and heat the air in winter.

There are electric wind-powered systems for homes and small businesses that have experienced growth over the last decade. The United States is the leading producer of small wind turbines. These machines are used to lower the electric bill and become free traditional sources of electric power. It costs about $40,000 for a 10-kilowatt system to be installed.

When purchasing appliances for a kitchen, think of energy conservation. Refrigerators use more energy than most appliances, so purchase one that saves energy. A self-cleaning stove uses less energy due to high insulation. If your client prefers a gas model, an electronic ignition saves energy compared to the constantly-burning pilot light. When designing a green kitchen for clients, you want to keep energy-efficient appliances in mind.

Green Education for Interior Designers

Talk with green vendors and see whether they offer any training seminars on their products. If so, set up a time for them to come to your office, or rent a room where you can invite other designers to come hear the presentation. Many manufacturers and vendors of green design offer information and training on how to use their products.

Consider taking green-related courses at your local community college and university. Many design schools have come up with courses to address the issue of green design. Some courses are continuing education, and others are credited toward a degree. Course content will vary, but might include waste and recycling, renewable energy, and green building design and construction. Some other topics to look for are lighting, selecting materials, energy conservation, sustainable materials, remodeling, and fabrics. There are online courses in green design offered by different organizations and colleges as well, for credit on topics like sustainability, environmental products, indoor air quality, and green materials. It can be a good way to take courses if you are busy and do not have time to devote to attending classes or seminars that last several hours.

If you have the time and the money to invest, you can learn quite a bit from seminars. They can be several hours to a few days long. The cost depends on location and topics covered. Seminars about how to build and design green might cover nontoxic materials, green roofs, understanding different materials and how to install them, solar energy, energy conservation, green textiles, furniture, and accessories. There may even be videos that you can watch to gain new information on green design.

For even more expanded education in green design, the San Francisco Institute of Architecture offers a master's in ecological design and architecture. Yale University offers a master's program in environmental management and architecture. And the ECOSA Institute[SM] in Prescott, Arizona, offers courses in sustainable and ecological design. Here, they get students from a wide range of design background, with instructors from the academic and design world. And the Institute for Sustainability maintains an updated list of colleges and universities that offer green courses. Maharishi University of Management, located in Fairfield, Iowa, offers a bachelor's degree in sustainable living environmental science. They teach people to design communities that meet the needs of people and the community — a holistic approach to teaching green design.

The U.S. Green Building Council offers workshops that discuss green building concepts.

Design Green offers continuing workshops for designers and others who want to learn to incorporate environmental awareness into their businesses. The Boston Architectural College offers on-campus and distance-learning courses in sustainable design. They also offer a Sustainable Design Certificate.

More About Applying Green Design to Rooms

There is a company that builds furniture from scraps of wood. Most of these scraps would be heaped in landfills, but the company gathers them from constructions sites and makes furniture. They use the scraps layered on top of each other to make furniture. Another manufacturer makes furniture from reclaimed flooring. Furniture can be made even from completely recycled plastics. Some companies use natural rubber latex foam for the cushions of chairs and sofas as an alternative to polyurethane-based fillings that have hazardous chemicals, and others design furniture that is cut to fit together without any bolts or glue — often, these are desks, bookcases, and file carts.

Bamboo grass is becoming a popular choice for furniture as a material of choice. The material, which harbors the strength of steel, can be woven into yarn to make bedding and manufactured into boards to make furniture, as an alternative to wood and plastic. Some furniture design companies have used bamboo to make kitchen cabinets using some new technology and engineering. It involves pressing them into a board like plywood to use in cabinets using nontoxic adhesives. Another company makes boards out of the sorghum plant grown in different parts of the world for food. Sorghum is a good substitute for wood and a beneficial use for the plant waste. One company turned coconut palm trees into wood used for cabinets. It is layered into sturdy, plywood-like boards, thus finding another used for the tree. The substances can be used for flooring and paneling.

Another innovative material is wheat board, which is a material made from wheat stalks and straw. Many of these materials are made without the dangerous chemicals used before. One company uses trees that have fallen from storms or will be taken down because of construction. Another makes kitchen countertops that look like granite but are made from 100-percent-recycled glass mixed with concrete. Some companies make countertops made of recycled paper and even aluminum.

Fabrics, which are used in every room, are an important part of green design. Some companies use organic cotton to make sheets, eliminating the pesticides used on the plant. Sheets, pillowcases, and other bedding are made from this material, and many conveniently come in wide selections of colors and patterns. Wool is pure material to make blankets and other coverings with. Sheet and linens made of bamboo are also popular. The Natural Bedroom is a company that makes mattresses of cotton, organic wool, hemp, and natural rubber latex from the sap of trees. Another manufacturer, called Lifekind®, uses natural rubber and organic cotton for mattresses and is Greenguard-certified. If you are furnishing a client's bedroom, think of using green products like these. The final touch is LED lamps with bulbs that last six times longer than traditional ones.

Cotton batt insulations are greener or environmentally friendly, as well as is sheep wool. They are the best of the fibrous insulation material. Foam insulation materials, like air krete, are green, as are perlite and rice hulls. Flooring material for design has many good products that are green like solid wood, bamboo, cork, natural linoleum, stone, and tile.

Bathrooms are another area of green design. One company designed a toilet with two separate chambers to flush different substances separately, a design that saves on water used in the bathroom. Another has designed a toilet that channels used water from a sink via a chamber for flushing. It is estimated to save about 5,000 gallons of water a year per household. Furthermore, there are energy-efficient showerheads that conserve water by injecting oxygen into the water. Tubs made of recycled plastics and polyester material come in many colors and simple designs. Towels are made with organic cotton, and some with cotton and bamboo are available for your very green-conscious clients.

Wall and ceiling covering experts are listing wallpaper and cork as the best green materials to use. Cabinets made of solid wood are the best for green design. Countertops made of solid wood, natural stone, engineered stone, and ceramic tile are safest for clients. Always think carefully about selections or products for green design — even trim should be solid wood or finger-jointed wood.

When designing a green bathroom, always keep in mind energy-efficiency and durable, safe materials. Bonded Logic insulation is safer and healthier than fiberglass, as you do not need a mask and gloves to install it into the walls. There is recycled tile, glass, and concrete that can be used for the bathroom installation or remodeling. Wood like maple, cherry, oak, and mahogany are also generally safe and durable.

Using as little water as possible is another consideration when designing a bathroom. Finding faucets and showerheads that are energy-efficient is important; for example, a dual-flush toilet will cut water consumption in your household. As an alternative to vinyl flooring, try tile or linoleum made of wood flour, resins, and linseed oil. These products are available in a variety of colors. Try using woods like bamboo, wheat straw, or sunflower plants. Counter tops made from recycled glass are a refreshing change. Try other alternatives to caulking used around windows. Having at least one window in the bathroom will provide ventilation and outside air.

Flooring has many green alternatives to consider if you are putting in new floors for your design project. Bamboo with no formaldehyde is durable and long-lasting. If you are looking for green carpets, look for those made of natural fibers or recycled synthetic fibers. Also look for the Carpet Institute Green Label Plus. If you use cork, look for products without formaldehyde, and try to avoid cork and vinyl combinations. Stone is a good choice of material for floors, as it is natural and highly durable. Tile and natural wood are excellent durable choices for floors in any office or home.

In the kitchen, energy-efficient hoods over the stove that remove fumes and vent outside are a good choice and can improve air quality in the kitchen. Gas stoves are not the best choice for green kitchens because they can emit nitrogen oxides, carbon monoxide, and sulfur. They also require more energy to run. Fortunately, new electric stoves are designed to be more energy efficient than older ones. Consider the differences when shopping for green appliances.

Insulate the bathroom well, and add radiant heat by adding heating tubes in the floor, the wall, and even a heated towel rack. Do not reuse old toilets; replace them with new ones that use less water. If you design a green bathroom, try to use an alternative to vinyl flooring, like tile or linoleum, available in a variety of colors. For wood, use harvested woods like bamboo, wheat flour, or sunflower plants free of chemicals. The walls can be covered in recycled glass, porcelain, or ceramic tiles. Always have a window you can open for ventilation.

Another new technology is a drain-water heater. This transfers heat from water going down the drain to the water heater, so it uses less energy to heat up water. The bathroom generates moisture that grows mold and mildew. Glass and ceramic tiles are good choices for floors and walls. They can be reused and are safe environmentally. Using un-sanded grout makes it harder for mold and mildew to collect.

The laundry room should be dry and moisture-free. If you need a sink, a cast iron salvaged sink may work in your laundry room. Front-loader washing machines are designed to save water by putting the drum on its side and tumbling clothes through a partially filled basin of water. They save water and use less detergent overall. Natural gas dryers are more energy-efficient than electric models. You should look for moisture sensor and automatic shutoff control. Metal duct vents are safe and durable, as they must be run to the outside.

As you can see, if you decide to specialize in green design, there is quite a bit to learn. Before jumping in and deciding you will specialize in only green design, do your research and find out whether there is anyone already doing this in your area, and if you do not find anyone, try to find out why. It might be that there is not enough demand in the area, or perhaps there is demand — and no one has tapped into this specialty.

CHAPTER 14

Preparing to Leave Your Business

At some point in the future, you will want to leave your business. You will either be ready to retire, or you will wish to sell the business and move on. The other choices include going out of business or leaving it to your heirs. When you are ready to sell, you will know why it is important to build a profitable, saleable business. When you start your business, you should also always be thinking about your future exit.

You can build a profitable interior design business with a loyal customer base and an efficient business structure that will earn you top dollar when you sell. You will want to consider the fact that with a design business, if you remain the only designer, you are the most prized asset. You will not have inventory and equipment as assets, but you will have the loyal customer base and solid business reputation that you have built for your design firm.

Exit Plan

Now is the time to develop an exit plan. You will not need as much detail for the exit plan as you needed for your business plan, but you want to develop it now and review it each year so that you can make any changes necessary. Your business situation will inevitably change from year to year, and you will want to revise your exit plan. Here are some of the basic items your plan should cover:

- **Your best-case scenario**: Do you know when you want to retire? Decide whether you want to sell the business or leave it for your family to manage.

- **Current value**: If you were to sell your business today, what is it worth?

- **Enhancing business value**: What changes would make your business more appealing for a buyer? Consider these carefully and realize that there might be some changes that you do not necessarily want to make, but that will enhance the value of the business when it is time to sell.

- **Worst-case scenario**: If you had to get out of the business today, what could be done?

- **Preparing for the sale**: You will want to be aware of the tax implications of the sale.

- **Leaving**: Are you in a partnership or corporation with others, and if so, how does this affect how you leave your business?

- **Financial health for your family**: Prepare a will. Is your family trained and prepared to run the business without you?

I would recommend that you meet with your attorney and your CPA for advice about how to create a realistic exit plan. To see some examples of exit plans, go to:

- American Express® Small Business: **www.americanexpress.com/smallbusiness**

- Principal Financial Group®: **www.principal.com/businessowner/bus_exit.htm**

- Family Business Experts: **www.family-business-experts.com/exit-planning.html**

Leaving Your Business to a Family Member

There are millions of large and small businesses that are operated by families. Some owners pass their business down to family members or heirs, and another option is to pass or sell the business to your business partners or employees.

There are tax implications if you leave the business to a family member. These issues include inheritance tax, trusts, and tax-free gifts. Each of these issues are complicated and you are advised to consult with your attorney, banker, estate planner, and CPA to make sure they are handled well. More resources include:

- The U.S. Chamber of Commerce offers advice at **www.uschamber.com**.

- CCH® Business Owner's Toolkit has articles to help you at **www.toolkit.cch.com**.

Selling to Your Employees

You might not have family members who are interested in carrying on the business without you, so you might consider selling the business to your employees. They will need to have adequate financing, and you will want to make it a professional transaction and include your attorney or accountant. Be aware that this can be highly emotional, as the employees buying your business might have different plans and ideas for how to potentially improve or change your business. The other issue is that it might feel uncomfortable to negotiate over money issues with friends.

Your employees might want to talk with a professional so that they clearly understand the transaction. For advice, see:

- The National Center for Employee Ownership at **www.nceo.org.**

- The Beyster Institute for Entrepreneurial Ownership at **www. fed.org**.

There are many ways to handle this transaction — including transferring your business to a worker co-op, or transferring directly to employees, similar to transferring it to family members — so it is a good idea to get advice and understand the process for everyone's sake.

Saying Your Goodbye

It is your business; you have built it from scratch. And even if you are tired and ready to leave, you might find it tough to give it up. Planning for this day in advance may make it a little easier because you will know that your business will be taken care of, and that all the work, struggle, sacrifice, and investment will not be lost, but preserved. If you have a plan in place, you will be creating a method and plan of preservation for this business that you worked so hard to build.

CONCLUSION

We have covered what it takes to be a designer, what it takes to be an entrepreneur, how to write a business and marketing plan, design trends, pricing, and more. We have included forms that you will find helpful, and even case studies of designers that are running a design business every day. Do not forget to review the forms on the accompanying CD-ROM — you can print them out and start using them immediately.

Running an interior design firm can be rewarding and fulfilling, but do not think it will not be hard work. It will require commitment, dedication, and ongoing education to stay on top of the trends. Customer service can be rewarding and exhausting at the same time. However, considering everything, owning and running my own design firm has been a most rewarding experience.

I hope that what you find in this book will inspire you and help you open and run a successful interior design business of your own.

APPENDIX A

Interior Design Forms

Design Master Room Sheet

Small designers often work on one room or a few rooms at a time in a home or at businesses. It is good to have a sheet that gives the details about each room of a project so that you know where you are with each phase of the project, room by room. It is usually filled out after the client and the designer have approved the work. The more details you have about the project, the better.

Design Master Room Sheet

Client_____

Room Worked On_____

Date_____

Floor Details_____
_____
_____

Wall Details _____
_____
_____

Ceilings_____

_____

_____

Window Treatments_____

_____

_____

Furniture_____

_____

_____

Appliances _____

_____

_____

Floors _____

_____

_____

Hardware _____

_____

_____

Lamps and Lighting Fixtures _____

_____

_____

Accessories _____

_____

_____

Art and Photography_____

_____

_____

Room Specification Form

This is a detailed description of the room and what will be done when the designer tackles the project so the client and designer can review the project. This form is helpful for the client to have and for the contractors working on the project, as it lists products and details so they will know how to proceed.

Room Specification Form

Room Specification_____

Client Name _____

Room Specified _____

Name of Project _____

Date_____

Carpet: Detail type and plan of installation_____
_____
_____

Walls: What treatment of wall paint, type, wall paper,
time schedule, and methods used_____
_____
_____

Ceilings: Paint used or work to be done _____
_____
_____

Windows and Treatments _____
_____
_____

Floors _____

_____

_____

Furniture _____

_____

_____

Built Ins _____

_____

_____

Lighting _____

_____

_____

Room Layout Dimensions _____

_____

Approval _____

_____

Research Sheet

Working on a design project often entails research, whether it is looking for merchandise in a catalog or calling vendors and suppliers for wood. You have to look extensively for special custom merchandise to order for a new business or home. This form gives you a place to document the information you find so that someone else not closely connected with the project can pick it up and find where the merchandise was found or ordered. It gives a detailed record of the project work and how it was handled.

Research Sheet

Client _____

_____

Date Assigned _____

_____

Due Date _____

_____

Staff Person _____

_____

Subject _____

_____

_____

_____

Goal _____

_____

_____

_____

_____

_____

Contacts _____

Results _____

Date/Time:

_____

_____

_____

_____

_____

_____

_____

_____

_____

Meeting Agenda

Interior designers often meet with clients and vendors to discuss the details of a design project. It is practical to have a form for meetings so details of the project can be recorded. Staff and vendors who are being paid for the project and for attending the meeting should be listed with time spent at the meeting and the total amount earned. Details and results of the meeting should be documented often.

Meeting Agenda

Date Scheduled _____

Time _____

Client_____

Locations _____

Purpose _____

Results _____

Schedule

Start	Stop	Total Hours	Start	Stop	Total Hours	Billing Rate	Value Per Hour	Total
Persons Attending								

Agenda _____

_____

_____

_____

_____

Items Required for Meetings _____
_____
_____

Persons Responsible _____
_____
_____
_____
_____
_____

Meeting Notes _____
_____
_____
_____

Decisions Made _____
_____
_____

Job Information Sheet

An important form is a job information sheet that tells you the details of
the design project, billable costs, profitability, materials and products used,
people working on the project, phases if the project is broken down into
manageable parts, implementation, fees, and costs. Below is a short form
that you may want to use as a template to design an individual form to suit
your project goals and needs. Many interior design companies specialize in
certain areas, so they must devise a form that reflects their specific needs.
This form reflects all time and costs that were part of the project. These
sheets can help you analyze trends, costs, profitability, and project types for
future needs.

Job Information Sheet

Name of Company _____

Job Name and Number _____

Location, Including Town and State_____

Client Name _____
Address _____
Phone _____
Cell _____
Fax _____
Any Other Contact Information _____

Bill-to Address_____
_____

Ship-to Address_____
_____

Project Team
Designer _____
Assistant Designer _____
Architects_____
Contractor or Subcontractors _____
Consultants _____

Billing Information
Rate_____
Time and Materials _____
Tax Percent_____
Total Cost _____

Design Development
Presentation Dates _____
Project Implementation Dates _____
Contract Document and Bids_____
Final Project Completion Items _____
_____

Work Change Order
Date_____

Number_____

Items_____

_____

Hours and Rate _____

_____

Expense _____

Items	Estimated Labor	Estimated Total	Actual Labor	Actual Material Expenses	Discount	Total
Floors						
Wood						
Tile						
Ceramic						
Carpeting						
Other						
Window Treatments						
Shades/ Blinds						
Louvers						
Draperies						
Fixtures						
Bath						
Kitchen						
Lighting						
Wall/Door						
Furniture purchased						
Furniture made or reuphol- stered						
Linens						

Rugs					
Appliances					
Insurance					
Storage					
Shipping					
Project Total					

Project Plan and Budget Form

This form helps you calculate the expenses of a project as an estimate. Many clients require estimates that often become contracts. It is helpful for designers who do not have much experience to provide detailed records of project and costs. If you do not have records of past projects, this form is a good one to use. Every project should have a paper trail. It is important to know which products and contractors are needed to complete a project successfully.

Project Plan and Budget Form

Client name _____

Address _____

City, State _____

Phone _____

Cell _____

Fax _____

E-mail _____

Estimating Format
Rates are by Hour, Day, or Week

Plus Expenses_____

Flat Fee_____

Program Development	ESTIMATE				COST					
	LABOR									
	Designer	Contractors	Design Asst.	Total Labor	Materials	Misc.	Budget	Balance	Allo-cated	Ba
Client Meeting										
Research										
Prelim Colors										
Budget										
Design Development										
Walls										
Floors										
Ceiling										
Window Treatment										
Fixtures and Hard-ware										
Furniture										
Design Phase 2										
Final Site Plan										
Final Layouts										
Revisions										
Final Budget										

Project Implementation	Fabrications Cus- tom Orders	Construction Site Supervision	Installation	Final Completion

Proposal Forms

The proposal is a targeted marketing attempt to win a project. Often it is used if other interior designers are competing for the same project. Sometimes it is used to persuade a new client to do a project that may be suited to them, but that they never considered before. It is detailed and tells the clients what you can do for them and how you plan to approach or target the project. Often, the form details terms and conditions of the project or how the design firm handles business for the clients. These forms can differ from design firm to design firm.

Proposal Forms

Date_____

Person Filling in Form_____

Client Information

Name_____

Address _____

City, State Zip_____

Phone _____

Cell _____

Fax _____

Project

Name_____

Location _____

Fee Information _____

_____

_____

Detailed description of the project _____

_____

_____

_____

_____

Work Plan Schedule	Start and End Dates	Budget	Notes	Total Time
Program Development				
Design Phase I				
Design Phase II				
Contacts and Documents				
Project Implemented				
Construction				
Installation				
Project Completion				
Work Plan Detail				

Wall and Ceilings	Notes	Budget	Total Time	Costs
Painting				
Wall coverings				
Moldings				
Other				
Floor/Stairways				
Wood				
Ceramic				
Stone				
Carpeting				
Moldings				
Other				
Window Treatments				
Shades/Blinds				
Louvers				
Drapery				
Other				
Millwork				
Fixtures and Hardware				

Bath				
Kitchen				
Lighting				
Wall/Door				
Other				
Furniture				
Furniture Purchase				
Furniture Commission				
Reconditioned Furniture				
Re-Upholstery				
Electronic Devices				
Spa/Exercise Furnishings				
Linens				
Rugs				
Decorative Items				
Miscellaneous				
Travel				
Messengers				
Insurance				
Storage				
Shipping and Handling				
Total				

Terms and Conditions

See Form.

Terms and Conditions

Change Orders: Work Change Orders will only be issued after discussion and approval of the client after work has begun. The client will be informed before additional charges are added or new material or work is ordered. The client will have to sign for changes and additions.

Purchasing: All purchases made will be billed to clients. Some costs, like insurance, taxes, shipping, and storage, will be added when deemed necessary. The designer is not responsible for quality of products received but will handle exchanges and returns when needed.

Deposits: At least a 50 percent deposit is required on all orders made on behalf of the client prior to the placement of such orders. The balance will be due upon delivery.

Custom Orders: The client is responsible for paying all costs of custom-made items. Payment must still be made, even upon cancellation of orders.

Termination Policy: Client and designer may terminate the contract based on agreeable terms to both parties.

The information in the proposal is valid for 30 days. When signed, the agreement is binding.

Designer Signature _____
Date_____

Client Signature_____
Date_____

Contract Summary Sheet

A contract summary sheet gives details of a project, like scheduling, purchases, contractors, and how the project will be completed. This form gives the information and details necessary to write up a contract for a design project.

Contract Summary Sheet

Client Name _____
Address _____
Cell Phone or Regular Phone_____
Fax _____

E-mail _____

Contact Person for Client _____

Designer _____

Detailed Description of Project _____

_____

_____

_____

_____

Project Beginning Date _____

Schedule of Project _____

How will merchandise purchased and construction costs be handled?

_____

_____

How will requests for additional work be handled? _____

_____

Estimated budget to be included with design concept. _____

Are revisions billable, and what expenses are billable? _____

_____

How long do you allow clients to pay bills after receipt of invoices? ____

Will you charge interest on overdue invoices? _____

What are the specific terms of the agreement? _____

Does the client want you to restrict publicizing the project? _____

Who will sign the agreement for the client? _____

Does the agreement have the following standard provisions for this design firm?_____

The quality and completion of merchandise is responsibility of construction, supplier, or contractor? *Yes or No* _____

If delays are cause by client, suppliers, or other acts, the timeline will be extended to finish the job? *Yes or No*_____

The designer shall have no liability for lateness, failure, or negligence of suppliers or contractors to perform duties? *Yes or No*_____

The clients will be responsible for payment of sales tax, packing, shipping, and related charges on such purchases? *Yes or No* _____

The client must sign and approve changes? *Yes or No* _____

The designer will own all rights to the designs? *Yes or No* _____

Is there an arbitration provision for problems that arise? *Yes or No*_____
_____

Person Completing Contract Summary Sheet _____

Date_____

Initial Survey Form

This form gives you an accurate picture of a site or area to be designed. It provides designs or drawings and a set of plans. The drawing and measurements must be as complete and accurate as possible, especially if this is a renovation or construction of a home or office building. Often, these forms are used by contractors and designers to complete the project.

Initial Survey Form

Client_____

Name_____

Project _____

Job Name _____

Location _____

Job Number _____

Site Dimensions and Conditions

Room or Site	Items	Drawing Number	Photographs Number	Notes

Inventory

Room or Site	Items	Drawing Number	Photograph Number	Notes

Date_____

By _____

Project Drawing Logs

Interior designers generate large amounts of paperwork when they work on projects. It is helpful to have logs for sketches, drawings, and presentations to keep track of the large amount of paperwork that is generated. It helps also to locate the drawing or sketch by knowing when it was made and logged in. Some projects generate a long list of drawings and sketches, so it is easier to have a log for each individual client.

Project Drawing Logs

Client_____

Name_____

Project _____

Job Name _____

Location _____

Job Number _____

Site Dimensions and Conditions

Room or Site	Item	Phase of Project	View of Drawing	Number	Location	Date	Notes

Contractor Log

Often, interior designers work with contractors to complete the jobs that they are working on. They work with plumbers, cabinetmakers, wood workers, architects, electricians, and other craftspeople. It is a good idea to have a log to keep track of these workers, especially for construction and special custom treatments, to list all contractors for one design project.

Contractor Log

Client_____

Name_____

Project _____

Location _____

Job Number _____

Item	Contractor	Contact in Organization

Bid Documents Spec	Drawings	P.O. Number	P.O. Total

Pricing Change Orders	Invoice Total	Schedule Start	Inspection	Delivery Date	Completed

Estimate Request Form

When you use different contractors for services, especially for custom work like cabinets, draperies, or furniture, it is wise to have an estimate form, as a practical way to obtain information for projects and decide whom to use. Some projects may require using different vendors or contractors, depending on their specialization, and some clients may request an estimate, too.

Estimate Request Form

Client_____
Date_____

Project Name _____
Requested by _____

Project Number _____

Phone _____
Fax _____
E-mail _____

Supplier or Vendor Name _____
Address _____
Phone _____
Fax _____
E-mail _____

Specifications and Descriptions of Services Offered

Item Number	Detailed Description of Items	Quantity	Unit Price	Total

Delivery Date of Services or Products _____

Subtotal _____

Shipping/Handling_____

Taxes_____

Total Estimate _____

Deposit _____

Date_____

Supplier Signature_____

Print Supplier Name _____

This is not a purchase order but an estimate of cost of services requested.

Purchase Order Form

The purchase order is a written document to vendors, manufacturers, and suppliers to either work on a specific assignment of a design project or deliver goods to the site. It is a record to the design firm of when and what has been ordered for a project and when the services will be executed. It is essential to retain digital and hard copies of purchase orders or have notebooks to put them in, as organization is important when completing design projects.

Purchase Order Form

Job Number _____

Date_____

Vendor _____

Address _____

P.O. Number or Address _____

Phone _____

Fax _____

E-mail Address _____

Contact_____

Schedule

Delivery Date _____

Installation Complete _____

Specifications of Merchandise or Service

Item Number	Description of Services	Quantity	Unit Price	Other	Total
					Subtotal
					Shipping/Handling
					Tax
					Total
					Deposit
					Balance Due

Notes_____

_____

Ship To:_____

Bill To:_____

Order by _____

Signature _____

Print Name _____

Phone _____

Fax _____

Project Status Report

Project status reports are important for interior designers who work on long-term projects. They keep clients informed of the company's progress on the project and the status. Some clients want regular status reports, especially if they have several contractors or vendors working on the project. These reports help maintain relations between vendors and clients. They help to keep the project on-track and resolve problems that arise. This form is helpful if you have new clients or those without much experience; it helps them to understand what is happening and in what order. You need cooperation from clients to complete a project correctly.

Project Status Report

Client Name _____

Job Number _____

Date_____

Job Name _____

Phase	Item	Status	Action Required	From	To	Date Due
Program Development						
Design Development						
Phase 1 Schematics						
Design Phase 2						
Contracts						
Documents						
Bids						
Implementation						

Work Change Order

When you are working on an interior design project, many times you will run over the budget or run into unexpected changes and expenses. It is vital to discuss any additional expenses and changes with the client before you go further. You will need a form and signature that details this information, as a record and to stay on track with your specific interior design projects. A brief, simple form is easy for the client to understand and sign.

Work Change Order

Client Name _____

Project _____

Order Number _____

Person Requesting Changes _____

Date_____

Job Number _____

Phase of Change _____

Program Development _____

Design Development Drawing and Schematics _____

Design Development Final Phase _____

Contract Documents and Bids_____

Implementation _____

Work Change Description Detailed _____

_____

_____

_____

Cost Change _____

Schedule Change Details _____
_____

This is not an invoice but a work change order; it represents changes from the original contact or order due to circumstances and must be based on the client's approval.

Authorized Signature _____
Print Name _____
Date_____

Credit Reference Form

Designers starting out in a business should look at a person's credit history if they are taking on a long-term project with high costs. When you look at a client's financial history, you can determine whether it is wise to develop a relationship or even offer a proposal to do a design if it is a client whom you want to acquire for future business. If you know vendors or suppliers who work with the client, call and ask them what they think of your client. If you do not know the client, you will have to ask for a list of credit references, which many designers do not want to do. It is important to do this, however, and to establish your business, you will have to do the same. Most vendors or suppliers will not work with you unless you establish your credit first. Not only should you get the information, but you should also contact the creditors of the new client. Most banks and credit organizations can supply you with the information that you need.

Credit Reference Form

Date_____

Company or Name of Client _____
Billing Address _____

Phone _____

Fax _____

Contact Person for Company _____

Companies _____

Number of Years in Business _____

Number of Employees_____

Number of Locations_____

Type of Business
Private, Incorporated, or Partnership

Federal ID _____

Individual _____

Employer Name _____

Address _____

Telephone_____

Years Employed_____

Home Own/Rent_____

Years at Current Address _____

Credit Agency	Telephone	Fax	Reference	Notes

Banks	Telephone	Fax	Account	Contact

Trade References	Telephone	Fax	Account	Contact

Personal References	Telephone	Fax	Notes	Results

By signing this form, you give the company permission to contact the listed individual to verify credit and financial information.

Company Name Signature _____
Date_____

Marketing Plan Form

Marketing is large part of promoting your business to get clients. It pays to have a form to document the work you do to promote or obtain new business. Calling former clients and potential new clients is important, but documenting the process gives you a record of results so you do not call the same person twice when they were not interested. Some of the best marketing tactics are word-of-mouth, personal introductions, and references from other happy clients. A log of calls made is a handy assessment of your marketing plans and goals. This form can be used on a weekly basis, if need be.

Marketing Plan Form

CALL LOG FOR MARKETING

Date_____

Company or Person Contacted _____

Title_____

Employee Making Calls_____

Purpose of Call _____
_____
_____

Notes on Call _____
_____
_____

Results _____

Marketing Actions Plans

Marketing is a big part of a successful interior design business. This form should detail your marketing plan, including logo, business cards, brochures, and methods of networking and promotion. The more details, the better; you can always go back to revise your plan as your business changes and grows.

Marketing Actions Plans

Date_____

Employee _____

Logo, Stationery, Business Cards _____
_____
_____

Brochures and Web Sites _____
_____
_____

Networking: Trade Show, Meeting, Cold Calls, and Chamber of Commerce _____

_____

_____

Written Communications Articles, Press Releases, Advertising, Newsletters, Surveys, E-mails, and Letters _____

_____

_____

_____

APPENDIX B

Financial Forms

Balance Sheet Form

A balance sheet will show you what financial shape your design business is in. If your accountant or bookkeeper does this aspect of your business, then you will have a good idea of where you are. This helps you make good decisions about purchases on merchandise or other aspects, like advertising and marketing. It also gives you an overview of your assets, liabilities, and the money available. The figures change weekly, so it is important to look at this sheet often.

Balance Sheet Form

Date of Balance Sheet _____

Name of Design Business _____

Account		Balance
Assets		
Cash in Bank		
Checking		
Savings		
Petty Cash		

Other Cash on Hand		
Accounts Receivable		
Office Furniture		
Less Depreciation		
Total Assets		
Liabilities and Equity		
Liabilities		
Accounts Payable		
Loans Payable		
Leases Payable		
Taxes		
Total Liabilities		
Equity		
Current Capital		
Current Net Profit		
Less Owner's Salary		
Total Equity		
Total Liabilities and Equity		

General Overhead Expenses		
Accounts Payable		
Advertising		
Automobile		
Phones		
Education		
Freight		
Insurance		
Legal and Professional Fees		
Miscellaneous Fees		

Office Supplies		
Phone Rental		
Referral Fees		
Rent Paid		
Samples		
Taxes		
Wages		
Bonuses		
Marketing		
Equipment Maintenance		
Postage		
	Total General Overhead Expenses	
	Net Profit Gross Profit Minus General Overhead Expenses	

Profit and Loss Worksheet

In a successfully operating interior design business, you will always have cash flow. You will have money coming in from your clients, and money going out to pay your bills and vendors. It is constant and will fluctuate according to the economic tides and other factors. It is a good idea to keep tabs on the financial pulse of your business; this is really the bottom line, no matter how successful you are. If you have no money in your account at the end of the month, then you can end up in a bind. Whether you have your accountant or bookkeeper do this or you do it yourself, it is important to monitor finances.

Profit and Loss Worksheet

Profit and Loss Worksheet for Dates Through _____

Income		
Gross Sales		
Other Income		
Total Income		
Cost of Sales Expenses		
Merchandise		
Manufacturer 1 Manufacturer 2		
Manufacturer 3		
Total		
Merchandise		
Manufacturer 1		
Manufacturer 2		
Manufacturer 3		
Total		
Merchandise		
Manufacturer 1		
Manufacturer 2		
Manufacturer 3		
Total		
Labor		
Manufacturer 1		
Manufacturer 2		
Manufacturer 3		
	Total Labor	
	Total Cost of Sales Expenses	
	Gross Profit	
	Sales Minus Cost of Sales Expenses	

CASE STUDY: JANE SPEROFF

Jane Speroff
Owner/Interior Decorator
INTERIORS by Decorating Den
11 Winhall Lame Trumbull, CT 06611
203-638-5108
Fax: 203-459-4897
www.decoratingden.com

Jane Speroff, Interior Decorator and owner of INTERIORS by Decorating Den®, has been in business for 3-plus years. Speroff's favorite type of project is when it is highly collaborative with the home owner. When presenting a proposed design to her clients, she usually creates with hand sketches and at times will use window treatment software tools to complete a design look.

When asked what a typical day is like, Speroff replied, "There is no typical day for me." Interior decorators' days can be endless and are always filled with a multitude of tasks, from running the business end of things, to sketching beautiful window treatment designs for clients.

CASE STUDY: JANE SPEROFF

Speroff made the decision to purchase a franchised company, INTERIORS by Decorating Den, primarily to have access to the volume pricing terms negotiated by the franchise with hundreds of vendors. She runs her business from a home-based studio and currently has no employees. Speroff's most successful marketing is networking and referrals. She says that it is "...very easy for me to build a relationship once I meet someone — and so being introduced or introducing myself is very effective for me. Direct mail has worked well in the past, but not so much in the current economic climate."

Living Room

Homeowners' goal: The home is one of those older ones with multiple rooms on the main floor that can serve multiple functions. When the homeowners first moved in, they were using this room as a catch-all space — mainly where the kids play — and across the foyer was the formal living room. They knew they were not using the spaces to their best advantage, but did not know how to re-configure things. This is a room that they wanted to use for entertaining, holiday gatherings, and quiet evenings after the kids went to bed.

Problem(s) addressed: This room was far too large and beautiful for a kids' play space. It has French doors to a deck, a large span of windows facing a wooded area, a nook — for who knows what — a fireplace, and some interesting built-ins. Neither privacy nor light control was needed. Seating for at least eight was needed for the holidays.

Solutions provided: We moved the beat-up furniture into the sunroom off the kitchen for the kids' room and started from scratch in this room. First, we created a large conversation area anchored by a big, square cocktail table and area rug with comfortable seating for six or seven people. Next, we added a bar and two bar stools in the nook at the front of the room. This allows for two additional people to sit. We added a leather bench under the large oil painting for yet more seating if needed. On the windows, we used unlined, relaxed Roman shades in a sheer linen fabric. The matching china cabinets with sliding doors not only make for beautiful display, but are large enough to store those pieces that are not used too often.

The built-ins accommodate special accent pieces and photographs nicely. The large oil reproduction piece sets a tranquil mood and draws the eye further into the room. The color palette reflects the shades of a beautiful New England fall — the couple's favorite time of year.

CASE STUDY: JANE SPEROFF

This is a room that will make entertaining, as well as quiet family time — a pleasure for years to come.

Parlor

Homeowners' goal: This is the same house as above.

Problem(s) addressed: This room was far too small for the dining room; the formal living room was never used. So we moved the dining room across the foyer and turned this room into an old-fashioned parlor. The room did not require any privacy or light control — it just needed to be beautiful and unique.

Solutions provided: Once this room was furnished with antiques and original art work and used as an adult sitting room, the windows needed to reflect the sophistication of the room's purpose. Because light control and privacy were of no concern, sheer fabrics were the answer. The panels are a cotton slub sateen with a sheer overlay — pleated together at the top only. The sheer shades feature a traditional vertical stripe pattern with beaded fringe along the bottom edge. The overall effect is as beautiful as a formal gown, but as fun as a prom dress.

Family Room

Homeowners' goal: The homeowners are a retired couple who moved out of their large custom home to another state and into a smaller, new-construction spec house in a development of similar homes. The pieces they brought with them were old and tired, and nothing worked in their new space.

This is the main room of the home, and so all the pieces need to be comfortable and inviting. Additionally, conscious of the fact that the outside of their home and the interior layout was the same as that of all their neighbors, they wanted their furnishings and the design of their room to benothing like those of their neighbors. Essentially, they want to be the envy of the neighborhood.

Solutions provided: Because the homeowners insisted they will never raise the shades because all they would see is the neighbor's house, we were able to put shades on the upper windows without needing to make them remote-operated. The swag, jabot, and panel design is intended to draw the eye up to take in the antique chandelier and the metal art work that fills the wall between the windows. The furnishings were all chosen with comfort and traditional style in mind. Two recliners are just what the husband and wife wanted for quiet nights, relaxing with each other, an afternoon nap, or a good book.

CASE STUDY: JANE SPEROFF

And when company comes, there is enough room for everyone to be comfortable. I have been assured by the homeowners that no one else in the development has a room that is as grand or beautiful as theirs.

CASE STUDY: RISSI CHERIE

Rissi Cherie
Owner/interior decorator
Rissi Cherie Decorating, Inc.
PO Box 1810 Interlachen, FL 32148
386-684-2650
Fax: 386.684.2650
www.RissiCherieDecorating.com

Opening in 2001, Rissi Cherie has been in business for eight years. As an interior decorator, Cherie's specialty is custom couture window and bedding fashions. she offers clients hand sketches of her proposed designs and is currently considering a CAD program.

Cherie's days are busy with phone calls to past clients and to vendors for follow-ups or orders, though most vendors are now requesting that you do business online. There is, of course, getting online and checking e-mails, sending e-mails, checking Web sites and blogs, and hoping not to get bogged down on the Web. The general office work of paying bills, filing, and planning ahead never stops. Then, there is working on the new project; this include working on design, products, availability checking, pricing, and double-checking the work to ensure not one detail has been overlooked. A good day is when there is the opportunity to make one or two client calls or to receive those new business calls from potential clients.

Cherie is an independent business owner. She was working for an interior decorator who had a small retail store. She decided to go out of business at the end of 2000. She was unprepared for that, but loved being an interior decorator. Upon short thought, excited about being her own boss and about having her own business, Cherie decided to become a business owner. She started without a dime, but her husband lent her $2,000 to start, and then it was learn, hustle, struggle, and never stop thinking about the business.

CASE STUDY: RISSI CHERIE

A slow start in the spring of 2001, followed by a back injury and the events of 9/11, made the first year difficult, but Cherie persevered.

Her business is home-based, and she has a small studio in a nearby town. Cherie has two freelance assistants, a bookkeeper, and her husband does installations and makes some small upholstered pieces that Cherie designs.

In regard to marketing, her ideas have ranged from door hangers; yellow-pages ads, which had value in the first few years but now have little value; ads in magazines; and PR pieces sent to the newspapers. Her biggest expense for advertising has been her Web page. Cherie says that she always ask for referrals, and there have been some good ones. This past fall, she held two decorator trunk shows featuring window treatments. As for marketing, she believe that branding and developing a niche are key to good promotion, as is face-to-face communication.

Cherie believes that some of the current trends include big-scale patterns in fabrics and wallpapers, unusual twists on old designs — sometimes Baroque — and sometimes, unexpected materials. Clients want something they can feel comfortable with, but yet something that has an air of being new and different. Beige is less coveted, for which designers around the world are no doubt grateful.

Project Details

The Project: A single woman's home, with emphasis on the living room, TV room, and Florida room.

The Problem: They had been decorated about five years earlier, and although there was some reference to her passion for butterflies, the decorating was stuffy and rather matronly in its execution and lacked style.

Goal: Play on the client's love of color, glamour, and brilliant blue butterflies to open up the rooms; add light and pizzazz; and express her personal and exuberant style.

For the TV room, we raised the draperies to ceiling height, extending their length with a contrast band at the bottom and tie-backs to allow more light into the room; added lighting at either end of the sectional sofa; and rearranged the accessories and pictures.

CASE STUDY: RISSI CHERIE

For the living room, we put in new, light gold carpeting, removed the valance and curtains at the only window, and replaced them with royal blue and gold silk draperies hung from custom, wrought-iron hardware. The arched openings to the Florida room were similarly treated, and those portieres added warmth and drama to the living room. A three-part arched mirror was hung, and a small, decorative table with a custom finish was placed in front of the window. Overall, we separated the room into three useful spaces: gathering area, reading area, and entry area.

The Florida room got new tile, a faux finish on the walls, and a Trompe l'Oeil design between the two arched openings. We added a rattan bar and stools and some new casual seating, creating a friendly, inviting environment.

CASE STUDY: VICKI MACENKA

Vicki Macenka, Owner and Decorator
Interior Transformations
6230 Stilegate Terrace
Mosley, VA 23120
Vicki@OneDayDecorator.com
804-307-4553

Interior Transformations does real estate home staging for clients. Vicki Macenka (**www.OneDayDecorator.com**) is an interior decorator with a Bachelor of Fine Arts degree from Virginia Commonwealth University. She is a member of the Interior Design Society and the Society of Decorating Professionals and is a certified Redesign and Home Staging Specialist.

Macenka says that before you sell your home, it is important to make it look as inviting as it can be so that you can sell it in the shortest amount of time. You want to present it so that the buyer will fall in love with the home. It is the psychology of selling your home. The emotions your home provokes will help sell your home. Most buyers want a home that looks and smells good.

Interior Transformations helps the client with changes in the décor. Sometimes it is just a small change, like cleaning and organizing. For a few hundred dollars, some wallpaper, lighting fixtures, and reduction of the visual distractions make a big improvement to the inside. Other times, just adding furniture or photos to the rooms or eliminating bright colors improves the appearance. They try to accentuate the architectural space of a home in a positive way.

CASE STUDY: VICKI MACENKA

They help the seller clear out all the clutter, which has a large impact when selling a home. Many people have too many accessories, toys, and furniture sitting around. When you remove the excess, you see a clean, uncluttered space. They go through the entire house room by room, as it is a powerful way to make a house more sellable. An orderly home makes a better presentation to the buyer.

Macenka's company sets the stage, decorates homes with furniture and art-work, and can create a conversation area to enhance a space if it will help sell the home. She helps homeowners clean out closets so they have room in them. Clutter can kill your chances of selling your home.

One-day decorating is another service she offers. She walks into someone's house who only wants one or two rooms decorated. Two people usually re-design the room, adding more furniture and creating a conversation area, for example. They sometimes re-hang art so it is more attractive and connected to the atmosphere of the room. They look through the entire home and sometimes bring artwork or furniture from the attic into other rooms if it creates a posi-tive atmosphere. Sometimes they buy new artwork, window treatments, or even greenery. They want to create a beautiful room for the client.

She has an office in her home with a sitting area, and she tries to give clients wholesale prices on some of the items she sells. She likes to find good buys for clients on a budget, while at the same time finding ways to decorate their homes with style.

CASE STUDY: ROBIN MCGARRY

Robin McGarry, ASID
Robin McGarry & Associates Interior Design
11 Riverfield Drive
Weston. CT 06883
203-454-1825, ext. 10
Fax: 203-454-9999
www.robinmcgarry.com

Robin McGarry & Associates Interior Design uses AutoCAD, which makes draw-ing more accurate and changes made more quickly. Robin McGarry does not use the program herself, as she still draws sketches on paper, but her intern uses the computer to draw the sketches into tight, professional designs for clients.

CASE STUDY: ROBIN MCGARRY

McGarry has a B.S. in Interior Design from Florida State University. She has owned Robin McGarry & Associates Interior Design in Weston, Connecticut since 1995.

A project will often take one to two years to complete. She always does an in-depth evaluation with new clients and will not evaluate a house or portion of a home without working up a detailed budget. She goes room-by-room and item-by-item when she does estimates. This can include all items in the room, including rugs, tables, and flooring. The budgets she works with range from $25,000 to $100,000.

The process of design often involves finding out what the client is willing to spend to achieve the look they want. She tries to educate the client so she does not spend time and money trying to find merchandise they do not want or will not pay for. She works up several estimates or numbers for the clients, giving them a good idea of what the design and renovation will cost. The floor plans include a detailed itemized budget.

The firm works on high-end residential homes, and she designs family rooms, kitchens, and many other types of rooms. Designers work from the inside out, while architects are trained to look at the outside and then go in. She says many architects are not familiar with the sizes and scales involving furniture and often build rooms that are suited to the furnishing of the house. She evaluates the design to make sure it works for the client in terms of furniture and the way groups of people gather in a room.

Sometimes she becomes involved with a design after the structure has been built. It can be challenging if the design does not work for the clients. Sometimes the firm has to do the design over, which is equally frustrating for the client. She finds residential projects more challenging than commercial projects because with homes, the designer must work with the emotions and belongings of the client.

She has paid for advertising, and the company's Web site draws many people with excellent photography of past projects. Because so many potential clients surf the Internet, this brings many callsfrom potential clients. McGarry gets referrals and repeat business from many clients because she has gained their trust; most of her clients come back every other year for a project.

She sees a current trend of people looking for tranquility and simplicity in their homes. The fast pace of a modern family's hectic schedules and information overload has created this need. Many clients are concerned with energy consumption and not putting anything in the home that is unhealthy.

CASE STUDY: ROBIN MCGARRY

She believes in charging for her design services and does not add a markup on furnishings. There is a debate in the industry on how to charge for interior design services, but her firm charges for its expertise in design.

She has a home office as well as a 12,000-square-foot commercial office space, and two employees: an office manager and a design assistant. She does residential and commercial work and has been profiled in many national magazines, and has participated in many community and civic activities.

CASE STUDY: RACHEL CLANCY

Rachel Clancy
RC Design
33 Calvin Street
Ayer, MA 01432
www.rcdesignonline.com
617-645-0606
978-772-6570

When you design with the correct design principles, any design, whether traditional, eclectic, or modern, will work more easily with clients, personalities, and lifestyles. RC Design designs primarily for residential homes, working with living rooms, master bedrooms, and kitchens.

One project Rachel Clancy worked on recently was a kitchen and dining room. The clients wanted to keep the existing cabinets, which were cherry, but cherry is a difficult wood to match and blend. RC Design broke down the wall for this project to combine the kitchen and dining room. They added a wet bar, workstation, and island to the new kitchen/dining room. As a designer, she has to know lighting codes, building codes, and how to work with architects. The trend is that the kitchens in many homes are getting larger.

RC Deign is a home-based business, and the successful marketing methods she has used for her business are a standard newsletter, word-of-mouth, and client referrals. She says she has little time for marketing. The RC Design Web site, featuring many photos of the work she has done, has brought many clients her way. Many people surf the Internet when looking for an interior designer, as she said she gets 30 percent of her clients through e-mails from the Web site, and the rest are phone calls. She says handing out her business cards is another inexpensive marketing tool. She belongs to a Women's Business Network, located in Harvard, Massachusetts, which is a networking group.

CASE STUDY: RACHEL CLANCY

RC Design worked on an entire Boston condo that was completed in two phases, involving designing and furnishing several rooms. The condo has a stairway the goes up to the deck and its results were so impressive that a movie scout recently looked at this condo as a possible location for filming a holiday movie with Sandra Bullock.

Clancy is also a member of the Boston Design Center, a retail center of more than 80 showrooms. The members are designers, architects, and other professionals. She often shops there for her clients because the center offers a wide selection of quality merchandise in different styles and tastes. Boston Design Centerfeatures cabinets, sinks, faucets, furniture, artwork, and accessories. Clancy works with a wide range of clients, from small projects to huge projects, and she likes to help someone on a budget benefit from her services without spending a fortune. She often gives discounts to some clients on certain items.

RC Design has been in the business for four years. Clancy's time has been spent setting up the business, getting clients, and developing a Web site with a local web designer. She recalls that her first project involved designing the first floor of a house, and it was an overwhelming project for a beginner. The completed project was featured on the front page of **www.carolinachair.com**.

She started using CAD for her designs two years ago. She says it makes a big difference in showing the clients the possibilities of layout, materials, and colors. It is easier to show the client different designs, and CAD makes saving and making changes faster. After a consultation, she will design a plan and use her laptop to show the client the results. It is easy to brainstorm and discuss the project with the client using the laptop, as she can print the plans and come back with fabric and colors to help sell or close the deal.

Clancy received her certification from Sheffield School of Interior Design in New York and is an associate member of the Interior Design Society. She is also a trade member of the Boston Design Center. Her services feature space planning, furniture selection, lighting, home office, home theatres, cabinetry design and details, and lifestyle definition.

CASE STUDY: NANCY MIKULICH

Nancy Mikulich, Interior Designer
NLM Design Interiors LLC
35 Charles Road, Building 1
Bernardsville, NJ 07924-1861
973-241-5151
www.nlmdesigns.net

Nancy Mikulich offers design and redesign services for clients who have food and chemical sensitivities. She works with vendors who sell green textiles and furniture to redesign rooms to be better for clients' health. She has a B.A. from New York State University and FIDER certification in interior design. She is a board member of a New Jersey chapter of interior design and has received an award for energy-efficient lighting design.

By attending seminars on green design, Mikulich stays on top of green design trends and uses the information for profitable design projects while making it affordable for the customer. She thinks clients will want more of this feature in the future.

Mikulich likes to offer green design because of her own experience with allergies. Nancy lived in the mountains near the redwood trees and on a river in California for 15 years. After losing her home when a giant tree fell on it and destroyed it, Mikulich has dealt with the complicated restrictions on rebuilding it and is now highly sensitive to ecological concerns. Her original home had redwood siding, and when they rebuilt the home, they had the redwood refilled and used inside the house.

Nancy has gotten business from referrals and from her Web site. She is trying to expand the scope of the services she offers to include green textiles and furnishings that other designers do not carry. She is working with a cabinet maker to design her own line of furniture and cabinets. This will distinguish her from other interior designers and make her more competitive.

Nancy says that green colors are subtle, and clients who want to make their homes a sanctuary seem to want to use more green colors. The fabrics are beautiful and the textures are muted, and the furniture is a classic, geometric modern style for green design. She sees a trend of furniture from 1950 through the 1970s coming back into vogue lately.

Mikulich feels that people are remodeling their kitchens and bathrooms more than ever before. They do not plan to sell their homes, so they are updating them. People are adding hardwood floors, tile to the bathrooms and kitchen, and new cabinets.

CASE STUDY: NANCY MIKULICH

She says it takes about three months to plan a design and often another three months to a year to complete the work; some projects take from six months to a year to complete. She does highly customized work for clients and has designed residences in California and New Jersey in all different styles. She gives clients detailed analyses, preliminary budgets, and detailed documentation of all projects.

CASE STUDY: LESLIE KLINCK

Leslie Klinck, Interior Decorator
Décor and You
Parker, Colorado
720-851-4233
lklinck@decorandyou.com

Leslie Klinck of Décor and You (**www.decorandyou.com**) runs an aggressive marketing campaign. She networks with business groups and often makes professional presentations, and runs advertising ads with profiles of her design team. Often, clients will relate to the designers, and many clients look for a personal connection when working with someone. Profiles of the decorators are a good advertising tool, as it is gives clients some personal background about the decorator. Many clients will say they saw the profile and say that is why they called.

Recently, Klinck participated in a women's expo that was an opportunity to talk and network with many vendors. She had a booth at the expo, which was a good opportunity to give clients and vendors a sense of who she was and what she did. Belonging to the local Chamber of Commerce is the key to building relationships with other businesses, as almost everyone knows someone who needs a room decorated or new window treatments. She meets once a month for lunch with the chamber groups and belongs to a few lead groups it hosts, volunteering to get herself known. She does as much as she can to be active.

The biggest part of her business is selling custom window treatments. She helps clients with accessories and furniture, too. Many people are moving into their first homes and need help making them look beautiful. She deals with blinds, draperies, valances, and shades. She says a window treatment can transform a room, and she works with many vendors who are introducing more green products, like flooring, window products, paints lower in VOCs, and furniture. The bulk of her business comes from networking, subscribing to ServiceMagic®, referrals, word-of-mouth, her own personal Web site, and the phone book.

CASE STUDY: CYNTHIA M. HERNANDEZ

Cynthia M. Hernandez
Owner & Principal Designer
INTERIORS by Decorating Den
45 Mountain Road
Farmington, CT 06032
860-838-1919
Fax: 860-674-6161
www.decdens.com/cmh

Cynthia Hernandez opened her business in 2007 and specializes in residential interior design. Hernandez decided to purchase an INTERIORS by Decorating Den franchise in 2007 after relocating to Connecticut. She decided to purchase based on her desire to change careers from the corporate world, but still have a corporate support system while she pursued her passion for interior design.

Hernandez works from a separate studio at her home. She currently does not have any employees; however, she does use the services of an accountant to handle taxes and to update her QuickBooks software as needed.

A typical day for Hernandez begins with time devoted to establishing the priorities for the day. Next is a check of e-mail and social media. Project design, ordering, follow-up — whatever is required on the to-do list is what gets done. Client appointments and installations are her first priority, so everything else is scheduled around them.

Hernandez uses multiple marketing channels, including referrals, direct mail, newspaper ads, social networking, her Web site, home shows, and social media. Referrals and the Web have been the most successful for her.

On current trends, Hernandez finds that neutral colors are still in vogue, but clients are branching out into new neutrals — grays, lavenders, blues — all in soft tones. There has been an increase in the desire for more formality, but not so formal that you feel you cannot sit in the room. Cynthia is convinced that the sloppy, slouchy sofa is a thing of the past.

Project Details

The Homeowner's goal: The family uses this room daily as their main living space, but also entertains frequently. Their goal for the space was a design comfortable for their own use that would also be welcoming to guests. Additionally, this is a family that reads considerably. They require storage for their many books, toys, and an accessible desk space for the husband.

CASE STUDY: CYNTHIA M. HERNANDEZ

All this, and a reconciliation of the husband's desire to live in an old English library and the wife's longing for an eclectic space — both vintage and modern.

Problems addressed:

1. Provide plenty of storage

2. Select new furniture that is "family room" comfortable with a "living room" look

3. Provide new window treatments to highlight the windows without blocking the view

4. Establish a design to suit both spouses' style sensibilities

Solutions provided: The one full wall in the room was not being used at all. Filling the wall with custom mahogany cabinetry addressed the storage needs, provided a home for the television, and set an undisputed focal point for the space that encompassed the fireplace. The traditional styling, custom cherry stain, and vintage-style brass sconces were met with both spouses' approval.

The existing rug set the color scheme for the space. The olive green, soft blue, and natural beige pulled from the rug combined in a soothing, neutral way without being bland. The new sofa has a vintage style with the modern comfort of down-blend seating and luxurious chenille upholstery. Though solid in color, the diamond pattern keeps the sofa lively. The armless chairs were chosen for their comfort and more modern silhouette, while their height contributes balance to that side of the room. The brass cube table is vintage 1940s. The armchairs provide lush comfort and the beautiful Chinoiserie fabric blends with the naturalistic vibe of the room. The large cocktail table and antique Chinese console table further ground the eclectic space. An ottoman serves as extra seating for guests. The modern secretary balances the cabinetry on the opposite wall and provides a work space with clean, sculptural form. Its lighter finish both complements and contrasts with the other woods. Accessories and artwork reflect the family's love of nature and the home's natural setting.

On the large window walls, neither light control nor privacy was an issue. The cornices were designed to draw the eye across the room to the outdoor view, without detracting from it. The olive and soft blue silks echo the colors of trees and sky outside. The integrated beading provides texture and a bit of understated glamour. Framing the windows with cornices provides architectural interest on both walls and lends balance.

CASE STUDY: CYNTHIA M. HERNANDEZ

The family tells me they love their new space. Their goals were met in a stylish way, and the new arrangements take full advantage of the room's size. Friends and family alike enjoy being enveloped by the room's warmth and comfort.

CASE STUDY: ALICIA STEWART

Alicia Fleury Stewart, CID, DDCD
Owner/Interior Decorator
Ali Stewart Designs/INTERIORS by Decorating Den
1904 Industrial Blvd, Suite 106
Colleyville, TX 76034
817-488-0034
Fax: 817-488-0063

Ali Stewart is an Interior Decorator who started her firm in 2005. She specializes in residential and light commercial projects. When creating designs for her clients, Stewart uses a combination of a Web-based room planner, Apple® Keynote®, and Dream Draper software to pull together her vision for the project.

When asked, "What is a typical day like for you?" Stewart shares that, "After arriving at my studio, I check voicemails and e-mails. I then start 'working my list' of all the things I need to accomplish. This is a master list, broken down into 'must-do's' for that day. Taking care of existing clients and their projects are 'must-do's.' After that, I try to focus on marketing, operations, and training (product knowledge)."

Stewart owns a franchised firm called INTERIORS by Decorating Den. After researching all possibilities of decorating franchises, Stewart felt that this company was a reputable, established company with a "turn-key" operation and automatic relationships with more than 100 vendors. They also had a sound, efficient, and proven business plan. Along with the rest of the benefits, INTERIORS by Decorating Den offered unlimited resources for training and operational support.

Stewart first started her business from her home, working in an at-home studio for the first year and a half, and as her business was growing, she decided to move it to a commercial space. She did not want a store front, so instead of retail space, she chose commercial space, which gives her more room and flexibility to house her samples, catalogs, and merchandise, as well as space for her three part-time decorators.

CASE STUDY: ALICIA STEWART

She mails a quarterly direct-mail piece focused on a more localized target market based on demographic information, such as home value and combined income. She likes face-to-face interaction, such as workshops, repeats and referrals, personal prospecting, and networking.

Alicia's hot design trends:

Dimension: Add some dimension by incorporating textural variety and tactile qualities in your room designs. Fabrics and rugs are now showcasing high-low weaves and cut designs.

Metallics: Copper, gold, bronze and silver threads can be found in a multitude of custom fabrics. Gold leads the way, but all warm metallics now have the spotlight.

Leather Looks: While leather and leather looks have been quite trendy the past few years, we are now seeing snakeskin coming on strong as a hot new look.

Retro: Splash patterns and motifs reminiscent of the 60s and 70s will be around for a while. For some, they will add a touch of nostalgia to room designs. And for others, these new, fresh colors definitely inspire the younger crowd.

Prints: Large-scale floral prints and traditional patterns are making a comeback — in colorful cotton blends, designed with an upscale, traditional look.

Architectural Accents: Many with a Moroccan and Moorish flavor, these accents feature arches, medallions, and fretwork in unique and classic wrought-iron designs.

Going Green: Today's environmental focus has increased interest in all things green, including the color green, as well as natural motifs.

Color

Green: Popular in many hues, green will shift to the cooler shades of two years ago, the only exception being a bright shade of yellow lime green.

Blue: You should expect to see more blues in general through 2010. Clean water blues and blues with a red cast are gaining. Teals will decrease, except for peacock, which will remain strong. Sapphire is bold and energetic and will be making a comeback, as will inky navy shades. New combo: navy and black.

Purple: Gaining ground, lilac and lavender are becoming mainstream, as are red-cast purples, like violet.

CASE STUDY: ALICIA STEWART

Hot Combos: Deep eggplant and wine; red-cast purple with chocolate brown; grey and silver paired with lilac; mauve was also making a comeback at market, in more modern hues and pairings.

Red: Watch for bluer shades of reds. Raspberry will stay on the cooler side for the next few years. Combos: Reds paired with oranges and golden hues.

Orange: Rusty shades and copper metallics will be big, as will warmer shades, from deep rust to corals to the softest peachy blush.

Yellow: Still gaining strength, especially yellows with a green cast. While bright yellows are no longer the current fashion, a more mellow yellow continues on in popularity, such as Pantone's Color of the Year, mimosa.

Brown: Holding on strong, chocolate brown looks delicious when paired with honeyed golden tones and metallic golds. Combos: Robin's egg blue and browns; browns and avocado; browns and ivory; browns and grey; and brown with blacks.

Grey: Peaking, and will move more into taupe shades, as well as steely blue tones and lilac grays. Sophisticated.

Black & White: Remaining strong — and not exclusively contemporary. Black paired with bright colors, like yellow or red, for punch, while black on black will continue to provide a very classic look and will often appear in matte and shiny combinations.

CASE STUDY: MARY LARSEN

Mary Larsen Designs andGrowYourDesignBiz
Owner
3340 Langston Circle
Apex, NC 27539
919-773-1445
www.GrowYourDesignBiz.com
www.MaryLarsenDesigns.com

"Mary Larsen Designs was launched two weeks after 9/11 in 2001. I'm sure that if I had talked to a lot of people and had sought out advice, I would have been strongly advised against starting a business at that time — but since then, I have learned that *not* following what other people think you should do is often the thing that works out best.

CASE STUDY: MARY LARSEN

The reason is simple — No one but you knows what you are capable of doing, how hard you are willing to work, and how creative you are willing to get to make your business a success.

So many people who get into the field of decorating do so because they love it. They love designing, working with a client, and helping people turn their homes into exactly what they want their home to be. This passion for your work will really make a difference in your business. When you love what you do, that enthusiasm is contagious; every project you work on will be infused with that enthusiasm, and it will give every project outcome that extra boost of something special.

The tricky part of your design business will be to pair your love of design and your love of what you do with the actual running of the business — because your business will not run on its own. Just because you are great at what you do and people will really benefit from your services doesn't mean that clients will just show up, or that you will even know how to most effectively run a project."

When Larsen first started her business, she focused solely on doing custom window treatment design and installation. Fabric and windows were her love, and she offered what she knew best. It didn't take long before Larsen's clients recognized her expertise in windows and then started to ask her what else she could offer them. Larsen learned pretty quickly that if more than three clients ask for something, it is time to seriously consider adding that service to your business.

Larsen read every book she could get her hands on and took many stand-alone classes on how to do residential interior design before she began offering it to her clients — she wanted to know why she was doing what she was doing that was design related so that she could communicate that to her clients. This process of getting educated so she could educate her clients has continued to work for her throughout her business.

Larsen had worked alone in my design business for a couple of years before hiring an assistant, and now cannot imagine her business without one. Larsen says that, "She can take care of so many things — like follow up — that really free me to spend time designing and working with my clients." Larsen opted to begin her own business rather than buy into a franchise because she is a complete do-it-yourselfer, and did not want to be tied down by rules that someone else created that were going to impact her business. Larsen works out of her home and says that she is grateful for that every day.

CASE STUDY: MARY LARSEN

She admits that she is "really good at separating work from home life, so the two don't really interfere with each other — but I have to admit, I love doing the laundry throughout my work day; folding clothes can be very therapeutic, and it often clears my mind and allows the creative work to continue — who knew!"

A couple of years ago, Larsen began teaching the things that she has learned in the design business and sharing that info with others through conferences and classes. Running a business is much different than doing design work. She literally spent thousands of dollars in her business trying to attract clients and found that much of the general small business advice did not apply to a home decorating business. For example, running a small ad in a local paper can cost a lot of money — and can often not result in a single client. On the other hand, working with a local carpet store to host an open house where you are going to speak on the seven hottest design trends — now *that* can land you a client, or four.

Speaking in front of an audience is Larsen's No. 1 favorite way to get new clients, and sending them an e-mail newsletter to stay in front of them on a regular basis is her favorite way to get repeat clients. Together, they work like a charm.

She uses this technique — speaking and then following up with e-mail newsletters — both for getting new design clients as well as getting designers who want help in growing their businesses; it is truly effective.

GLOSSARY

#

360-Degree Feedback: A method in which an employee may receive feedback on his or her own performance from a supervisor and up to eight co-workers, reporting staff members, or customers.

A

Absence or Absent (Scheduled): A period of time off from work that is previously planned during a normally scheduled work period.

Absence or Absent (Unscheduled): A period of time off from work during a normally scheduled work period that has not been planned.

Absenteeism Policy: A policy that provides guidance within an organization regarding management of an employee's chronic absence from work.

Absorptive Capacity: The ability of a company to identify, value, assimilate, and use newly acquired knowledge.

Acquisitions: The strategy a company uses to enter a new business area and develop it by buying an existing business.

Adaptive Cultures: The environment within a company where innovative employees are encouraged, and initiative is awarded by middle- and lower-level managers.

Attendance Policy: The expectations and guidelines for employees to report to work as written, distributed, and enforced by an organization.

B

Background Checking: The act of looking into a person's employment, security, or financial history before offering employment or granting a license.

Behavioral Interview: An analysis of answers to situational questions that attempts to determine if you have the behavioral characteristics that have been selected as necessary for success in a particular job.

Benefits: Additions to employees' base salary, such as health insurance, dental insurance, life insurance, disability insurance, a severance package, or tuition assistance.

Bereavement Policy: The portion of an employment contract that provides for a certain amount of time off from work when an employee's spouse or close family member passes away.

Bonus Plan: A system of rewards that generally recognizes the performance of a company's key individuals, according to a specified measure of performance.

Bottom-Up Change: A gradual process in which the top management in a company consults with several levels of managers in the organization and develops a detailed plan for change with a timetable of events and stages the company will go through.

Broadbanding: A salary structure in which pay ranges are consolidated into broader categories to reduce overlap with other pay ranges.

C

Capabilities: The skills a company has in coordinating its resources efficiently and productively.

Cash Flow: The amount of cash a business, receives minus cash, that must be distributed for expenses.

Centralization: A type of hierarchy in an organization in which upper-level managers have the authority to make the most important decisions.

Clarity of Expectations: The concept that before, during, and after strategic decisions are made, managers should have a clear understanding of what is expected of them, as well as an idea of any new rules or strategies.

Coaching: A method used by managers and supervisors for providing constructive feedback to employees in order to help them continue to perform well, or to identify ways in which they can improve their performance.

Cognitive Bias: Errors in the methods human decision-makers use to process information and reach decisions.

Commission System: A system of rewards in which employees are paid based on how much they sell.

Company Infrastructure: A work environment in which all activities take place, including the organizational structure, control systems, and culture.

Conflict Aftermath: The long-term effects that emerge in the last stage of the conflict process.

Congruence: The state in which a company's strategy, structure, and controls work together.

Corporate Governance: The strategies used to watch over managers and ensure that the actions they take are consistent with the interests of primary stakeholders.

Counseling: The act of providing daily feedback to employees regarding areas in which their work performance can improve.

Cycle: An iteration of the planning process that begins with the corporate mission statement and major corporate goals.

D

Decentralization: An organizational hierarchy in which authority has been delegated to divisions, functions, managers, and workers at lower levels in the company.

Devil's Advocacy: A way of improving decision making by generating a plan and a critical analysis of that plan.

Dialectic Inquiry: A way to improve decision making by generating a plan and a counter-plan.

Differentiation: The method a company uses to allocate people and resources to certain tasks in the organization to create value.

Discipline: A process of dealing with job-related behavior that does not meet communicated performance expectations.

Diversification: The process of entering into new industries or business areas.

Division: The portion of a company that operates in a particular business area.

Downsizing: The process of reducing employee headcount in an organization.

Dress Code for Business Casual: A company's objective to enable employees to project a professional, business-like image while experiencing the advantages of more casual and relaxed clothing.

E

Efficiency: The measurement derived from dividing output by input.

Emotional Intelligence: A term that describes a bundle of psychological characteristics that many strong leaders exhibit (self-awareness, self-regulation, motivation, empathy, and social skills).

Empathy: The psychological characteristic that refers to understanding the feelings and viewpoints of subordinates and taking them into account when making decisions.

Employee Empowerment: The process of enabling or authorizing an individual to think, behave, take action, and control work and decision-making autonomously.

Employee Involvement: The act of creating an environment in which people may take part in decisions or actions that affect their jobs.

Employee Stock Option Plan (ESOP): A system of rewarding employees in which they may buy shares in the company at below-market prices.

Employment Eligibility Verification (I-9): The form required by the Department of Homeland Security U.S. Citizenship and Immigration Services to document an employee's eligibility to be employed in America.

Engagement: The process of involving individuals in active decision making by asking them for their input and by allowing them to refute the merits of one another's ideas and assumptions.

Exempt Employee: Employees who are not confined by the laws governing standard minimum wage and overtime.

Explanation: The idea that all those who are involved and/or affected should be told the basic reasoning for strategic decisions and why some ideas and inputs may have been overridden.

F

Fair Labor Standards Act (FLSA): The legislation that requires a company to pay a nonexempt employee who works more than a 40-hour week 150 percent of their regular hourly rate for the overtime hours.

Family and Medical Leave Act (FMLA): The legislation that states that covered companies must grant an eligible employee up to 12 weeks of unpaid leave during any 12-month period of time for one or more of the covered reasons.

Feedback: The information given to or received from another person regarding the impact of their actions on a person, situation, or activity.

Felt Conflict: The type of conflict occurring at the stage in which managers start to personalize the disagreement.

Franchising: A business strategy in which the franchisor grants the franchisee the right to use the parent company's name, reputation, and business skills at a particular location or area.

Functional Structure: An organizational method of grouping people based on their common expertise and experience or on the same set of resources those people use.

G

Garnishment: A legal procedure in which a person's earnings are withheld by an employer for the repayment of a debt.

General Manager: A person who bears all responsibility for the organization's overall performance or that of one of its major self-contained divisions.

Goal: The future state a company attempts to reach.

H

Horizontal Differentiation: The way in which the company focuses on the grouping of people and tasks into functions and divisions to meet the objectives of the business.

Human Resources: (1) The people who are part of an organization and its operations. (2) The business function that deals with the employees of a company.

I

Independent Contractor: A person or a business that performs services or supplies a product for a person or a business under a written or implied contract.

Industry: A group of companies that offer products or services that are similar to each other.

Integration: The process by which a company coordinates people and functions to accomplish certain tasks within the organization.

Internal Governance: The way in which the top executives in a company manage individuals within the organization.

J

Job Offer Letter: A written document that confirms the details of an offer of employment, including details such as the job description, reporting relationship, salary, bonus potential, and benefits.

L

Labor-Management Glossary: A comprehensive list of the definitions of labor management terms provided by the U.S. Office of Personnel Management.

Learning Effects: The cost savings that come from learning while performing the task.

Legitimate Power: The authority a manager holds due to being placed in a formal position in the organization's hierarchy.

M

Management by Objectives (MBO): A process in which managers participate in their evaluation of their capability to achieve certain organizational goals or performance standards and to meet the given operating budget.

Marketing Strategy: The stand a company takes regarding pricing, promotion, advertising, product design, and distribution.

Minimum Wage: The minimum amount of compensation per hour for covered, nonexempt employees as defined by the Fair Labor Standards Act (FLSA) and by local states.

Mission Statement: A brief but precise definition of what an organization does and why.

Motivation: A psychological portion of emotional intelligence that refers to a passion for work that goes beyond money or status and enables a person to pursue goals with energy and persistence.

N

Negativity: The concept and expression of unhappiness, anger, or frustration to other employees in the workplace.

Networking: The act of building interpersonal relationships that could be mutually beneficial.

New Employee Orientation: Also call Induction. The process of orienting a new employee to a company, usually performed by one or more representatives from the human resource department.

Non-Exempt Employee: Employees who are protected by the laws governing standard wages and overtime.

O

Occupational Outlook Handbook: A nationally recognized source of career information that is designed to provide assistance to individu-

als who are making decisions about their careers.

Operations Manager: An individual who is responsible for particular business operations.

Optimism: The ability or tendency to look at the positive side of a situation or to expect the best possible results from any series of events.

Organization Bonus System: A system of rewards based on the performance measurement of the organization during the most recent time period.

Organizational Politics: The strategies that managers use to obtain and use power in order to influence business processes to further their own interests.

Organizational Values: Concept regarding the goals that individuals within an organization should pursue and what behavioral standards they should follow to achieve these goals.

Orientation: See New Employee Orientation.

Outsourcing: The act of paying another individual or business to perform certain internal processes or functions.

P

Perceived Conflict: Conflict that occurs when managers are made aware of clashes within an organization.

Performance Management: A policy for dealing with behavior on the job that does not meet expected and communicated performance standards.

Piecework Plan: A system of rewards in which output can be accurately measured, and employees are paid based on a set amount.

Profit-Sharing System: A system of rewards that compensates employees based on the company's profit during a specified time period.

Progressive Discipline: A process for dealing with behavior on the job that does not meet expected and communicated performance standards.

Project Management: The process of applying knowledge, skills, tools, and techniques to a wide range of activities in order to meet the requirements of the particular project.

Promotion: The act of advancing an employee to a position with a higher salary range maximum.

Q

Quality: A measurement of excellence in the desirable characteristics of a product, a process, or a service.

R

Recognition: A practice of providing attention or favorable notice to another person.

Recruiters: People who are hired by a company to find and qualify new employees for the organization.

Restructuring: A method of improving company performance by reducing the level of differentiation and downsizing the number of employees to decrease operating expenses.

S

Screening Interview: A quick, efficient discussion used to qualify candidates before they meet with the hiring authority.

Self-Awareness: The psychological characteristic of a person's emotional intelligence in which he is able to understand his own moods, emotions, drives, and his effect on others.

Self-Discipline: The psychological ability to control one's own behavior.

Self-Regulation: The psychological ability to control or redirect one's own disruptive impulses or moods.

Sexual Harassment: The act of an employee's making continued, unwelcome sexual advances, requests for sexual favors, and/or other verbal or physical conduct toward another employee against her/his wishes.

Sexual Harassment Investigation: The process of looking into an employee's complaint of sexual or other harassment in the workplace.

Social Skills: The psychological ability to interact purposefully with others at a friendly level.

Span of Control: The number of employees a manager manages directly.

Strategic Control: The process in which managers monitor an organization's ongoing activities, members, and correct performance as necessary.

Strategic Control Systems: Formal systems for target setting, measurement, and feedback that allow managers to evaluate whether a company is achieving top efficiency, quality, innovation, and customer responsiveness, and implementing its strategy successfully.

Strategic Leadership: The charisma of someone that enables him or her to articulate a strategic vision for the company or part of the company and motivates others to share that vision.

Strategic Management Process: The process in which a set of goals or strategies is chosen by managers for the enterprise.

T

Top-Down Change: An adjustment that occurs when a strong upper-management team analyzes how to alter strategy and structure, recommends an appropriate course of action, and moves quickly to restructure and implement change in the organization.

Total Quality Management (TQM): A philosophy of management that concentrates on improving the quality of a company's products and services and stresses that all operations should head toward this goal.

Two-Boss Employees: Employees who work on a project-based team and are responsible for coordinat-

ing and communicating among the functions and projects.

U

Unemployment Compensation: A policy created by the Social Security Act of 1935 to protect workers who lost their jobs due to circumstances outside their own control.

V

Values: Traits or characteristics that are considered to be worthwhile and that represent an individual's priorities and driving forces.

BIBLIOGRAPHY

Crawford, Tad & Bruck, Eva,D.; Business and Legal for Interior Design, Allworth Press, New York, 2001

Dorfman, Josh & Abrams, Harry, N., The Lazy Environmentalist, Your Guide to Easy Stylish Green Living, Inc. 2007

Gilliatt, Mary, Designing Rooms for Children, Little Brown and Company, 1984

Gross, Scott, T., Positively Outrageous Customer Service, Warner Books, 1991

Knackstedt, Mary, V., The Interior Design Business Handbook, Fourth Edition, John Wiley and Sons, 2005

Levinson, Conrad, J.; Frishman, Rick & Lublin, Jill, Guerrilla Publicity, Adams Media Corporation, 2002

McCorquodale, A History of Interior Design for Rhodec University, 2007

Phillips, Nita, How to Start a Home-Based Interior Design Business, The Globe Pequot Press, 2006

Ries, Al & Trout, Jack, Positioning-The Battle for Your Mind, Warner Books, 1993

Venolia, Carol & Lerner, Kelly, Natural Remodeling for the Not-So-Green House, Lark Books, 2006

Vila, Bob & Howard, Hugh; Bob Vila's Complete Guide to Remodeling Your Home: Everything You Need to Know about Home Renovations From the #1 Home Improvement Expert, Avon Books, 1999

Williams, Stephen, The Interior Designer's Guide to Pricing, Estimating and Budgeting, New York, 2005

Maxey Hayse Design Studios, Copyright 2006, **www.maxeyhayse.com/ maxeyhayse_sitemap.html**

Hospitality Design Magazine, **www.hdmag.com**

Green Building Council, **www.buildgreenschools.org/gs101/**

The Top Ten Green Schools in US, National Geographic, July/August 2006, **www.thegreenguide.com/doc/115/toptenschools/6**

IBIS World http://ibisworld.ecnext.com

Green Home Guide Web site, **www.greenhomeguide.com**

American Marketing Association Releases New Definition of Marketing, January 14, 2008, **www.btobonline.com/apps/pbcs.dll/ article?AID=/20080114/FREE/454122962/1078/newsletter01**

Dorothy Draper Web site, February 5, 2009, **www.DorothyDraper.com**

Design Within Reach Web site, February 5, 2009, **www.DesignWithin-Reach.com**

Barbara Berry Web site, February 5, 2009, **www.BarbaraBerry.com**

Nate Berkus Web site, February 5, 2009, **www.nateberkus.com**

Vern Yip Web site, February 5, 2009, **www.vernyip.com**

Candice Olsen Web site, February 5, 2009, **www.divinedesign.tv/master.asp**

NASAA Web site, February 5, 2009, **www.nasaa.org**

Leone, Dianae. "Top Five Interior Designers in the United States." National Examiner. September 30. **www.examiner.com/x-564-Interior-Design-Examiner~y2008m9d30-Top-Five-Interior-Designers-in-the-United-States**

SUGGESTED READING

Atlantic Publishing Group, Inc. offers a book titled *How to Get the Financing for Your New Small Business: Innovative Solutions from the Experts Who Do It Everyday* (**www.atlantic-pub.com,** ISBN: 978-0-910627-55-9). Insufficient financing can be fatal to a new business. This book shows you ways to secure sufficient financing for your business and discusses topics that include detailed valuations and proper funding projections, and it gives illustrations of various types of financing options that might be available.

On the accompanying CD-ROM, you will find a Word document that has a template of a business plan that you can use to develop your plan. You can insert the specific information for your design business. Atlantic Publishing offers a good resource for writing business plans: *How to Write a Great Business Plan for Your Small Business in Sixty Minutes or Less* (**www. atlantic-pub.com,** ISBN: 978-0-910627-56-6).

For assistance in planning for how to get the best price for your business when you are ready to sell, Atlantic Publishing offers a book titled *How to Buy and or Sell a Small Business for Maximum Profit – A Step-by-Step Guide* (**www.atlantic-pub.com,** ISBN: 978-0-910627-53-5). This book offers tips on how to get the best price for your business and helps you understand the paperwork and the laws that will affect you when you sell or buy a business.

Also available from Atlantic Publishing is *How to Open and Operate a Financially Successful Redesign, Redecorating and Home Staging Business* (**www. atlantic-pub.com**, ISBN: 978-1-601380-23-4). It offers a practical, step-by-step plan for launching your business and keeping your business growing. Using tested and proven methods that apply specifically to the business of design, this book will help you discover the most effective means to attracting clients to your design services and generating income fast. The accompanying CD, with checklists, forms, templates and samples are available for free download.

AUTHOR BIOGRAPHY

Diane Leone is a native of St. Augustine, Florida. Diane is a Certified Interior Decorator and owns her own design firm. She is also a marketing specialist and has owned her own marketing firm, Marketing Edge, Inc., for the past 15 years. Diane is also an established author with a published marketing book, *Marketing Multifamily Housing with Integrated Marketing Strategies*, available at **www.amazon.com**.

Diane currently writes a monthly column on design trends for a regional magazine, as well as a monthly column on the business of design for a national magazine. Diane's background includes marketing, advertising, television, radio, agency work, event and wedding planning, writing, and interior decorating. Diane has hosted several local real estate design shows.

Diane's business was honored as one of the Top 100 Fastest Growing Businesses in the State of Florida in 1999. She has a passion for education and was appointed by the Governor to serve on two State Educational Advisory Boards, the Postsecondary Education Advisory Council, and The Council for Education Policy Research and Improvement, and she currently serves on the Board of Trustees for St. Johns River Community College.

For more information about Diane's work, visit her Web site at **www.DianeLeone.com.**

INDEX

12-10-10

4-22-15

4

3